To Marie,

A review of the architecture and sculpture in Philadelphia, Pennsylvania, U.S.A.

From June

February, 1988

Fairmount, Philadelphia's Park

PLATE 1. Waterworks and museum. *Photograph by Charles F. Ward, Jr.*

Fairmount, Philadelphia's Park

A History

Theo B. White

Photography by George E. Thomas

Philadelphia: The Art Alliance Press
London: Associated University Presses

Associated University Presses, Inc.
Cranbury, New Jersey 08512

Associated University Presses
108 New Bond Street
London W1Y OQX, England

Library of Congress Cataloging in Publication Data

White, Theophilus Ballou, 1903—
    Fairmount, Philadelphia's park.

    Bibliography: p.
    Includes index.
       1. Philadelphia—Parks—Fairmount Park—History.
I. Title.
F158.65.F2W4   974.8'11   75-8128
ISBN 0-87982-015-2

*The preparation of this book was made possible
by a grant from the Johnson Research Fund of
the American Philosophical Society.*

PRINTED IN THE UNITED STATES OF AMERICA

For
my wife, Anne,
and
David M. Robb
George B. Tatum
George E. Thomas

Contents

List of Illustrations

Preface

I suspect that my first interest in Fairmount Park was stirred when as a young man I attended a dinner of the American Institute of Architects at which Mr. Charles D. Maginnis, president of the institute and a distinguished architect in Boston, spoke. In his opening remarks he said in effect that it was a pleasure to enter Philadelphia by train from the north because one slowly crossed the Schuylkill and came into the city through Fairmount Park. He further said that the citizens of the city could be justly proud of the park.

I am quite sure we are.

Since then I have ridden horses in the park, I have paddled a canoe on the Schuylkill, and have many times walked the Wissahickon, ending up at Valley Green Inn for a sandwich and tea. And finally, my architectural firm has frequently been commissioned for improvements and buildings in the park.

I have come to love the park and hence this book about it — a book I have for some years wanted to do.

In the preparation of this book I have encountered enthusiastic assistance from many people to whom I want to express my appreciation. Dr. David M. Robb, professor emeritus of the University of Pennsylvania has read the manuscript and made excellent suggestions. Dr. George B. Tatum of the University of Delaware has kindly allowed me to reprint his paper on the Centennial. Mr. George E. Thomas of the University of Pennsylvania has furnished me photographs from his collection and added new ones; these I think are splendid.

Dr. John McDonogh of the Library of Congress kindly gave me access to the collection of papers of Frederick Law Olmsted. Mr. Ward Childs in the Archives of City Hall was most helpful in furnishing me the volumes of the minutes of the Park Commission. Mr. Edwin Wolf, II, librarian of the Library Company of Philadelphia and his assistants Mrs. Lillian Tonkin and Miss Julia Goscinski were most cooperative in placing books and maps at my disposal. Mrs. Eileen Wilson of the Fairmount Park Art Association loaned me documents of the association, as did Mr. Richard Cooper and Miss Jean Verlender of the Zoological Society. Mr. Anthony Walmsley loaned me the photograph of Frederick Law Olmsted.

Finally, I am deeply grateful to my wife for her encouragement and criticism.

Theo B. White
Villanova

Fairmount, Philadelphia's Park

1

The Banks of the Schuylkill

From the minutes of a meeting of the Commissioners of Fairmount Park in 1868:

The ground we propose to acquire is peculiarly adapted to Park purposes. No other city in the Union has within its boundaries, streams which, in picturesque and romantic beauty, can compare with the Wissahickon and the Schuylkill; and there are few which include within their limits landscapes which, in sylvan grace and beauty, surpass those which abound within the spaces we propose to appropriate. Nature herself has so adorned them that little remains for art to do except skillfully develop the natural beauties of the ground. Here through long coming generations . . . will this Park continue—a monument of wisdom and the foresight of those who founded it—protecting the purity and securing the abundance of their water supply; ministering in its clear air and ample grounds to their health and enjoyment and in the beauty and grace of its natural and its artificial adornments to the refinement of their taste; while to the spots already of historic interest, which are within its bounds, will be added others on which stately buildings will arise, for works of art or taste, or for instruction in natural science, or where monuments will be reared to the immortal memory of those who in their day have greatly served the State.

An Act of the General Assembly dated March 26, 1867, approved the boundaries of Fairmount Park and invested title and ownership in the City of Philadelphia, and further stated that the city was empowered to "appropriate and set apart forever the area of land and water comprised within the limits . . . as open public ground and Park for the *preservation of Schuylkill water* [my italics] and of the health and enjoyment of the people forever."

Although the year 1867 was a notable and productive one, the city had as early as 1812 acquired land to secure good water "free from impurities of City drainage and a site for a reservoir high enough to distribute water to the tallest buildings in town." Such land had been known as *Faire-Mount* and was outside the city limits. It is now the site of the Art Museum, the bowels of which reach down to the bottom of the reservoir. Ground for the waterworks was acquired in three parcels in 1812, 1815, and an unknown date for the third parcel. The first two pieces cost $16,600 each and the third $12,000. This comprised 24 acres by 1828. The vista up the river valley from this land included Lemon Hill and Sedgley on the east bank (Plate 2) and Solitude, Egglesfield, and Lansdowne on the west bank. There was no town on the river until the *village* of Norristown, some 15 miles up the river.

The waterworks, built in 1819-1822 by Frederick Graff, an apprentice of Latrobe, lasted for some 30 years before the city discovered that "their cup of water was in danger of becoming a poisoned chalice." It is truly a wonder that the early nineteenth-century waterworks functioned that long, particularly in view of the rapid growth of the city and its expanding population.

In a meeting of the commissioners in January 1868, it was recorded that "this water supply [Schuylkill] hitherto of unsurpassed abundance, and of unequalled purity—is adequate for the prospective wants of the people for generations to come, if proper economy is observed . . . and *proper provision is made to protect, and preserve its purity* [my italics]."

Thus, in that last sentence is the compelling reason for the establishment and preservation of the early parts of Fairmount Park. All sentiments and enthusiasm about the value of it as a place of recreation are quite true; but the basic fact emerges that the city fathers and the Fairmount Park commissioners were desperately in need to preserve the river as a source of palatable and healthful water supply to a city that was rapidly expanding, both geographically and in its population.

This, then, is the really practical reason for the founding and, for a number of years, the maintenance of Fairmount Park. The fine-sounding sentiments in the first paragraph of this chapter with regard to the sociological advantages of a park were really, in truth, just words, compared to the real and vital reasons for the preservation in clean decency and

PLATE 2. Plan by Frederick Graff dated 1851. It is possible that Graff foresaw this area as a public park and so made a plan of it as a record.

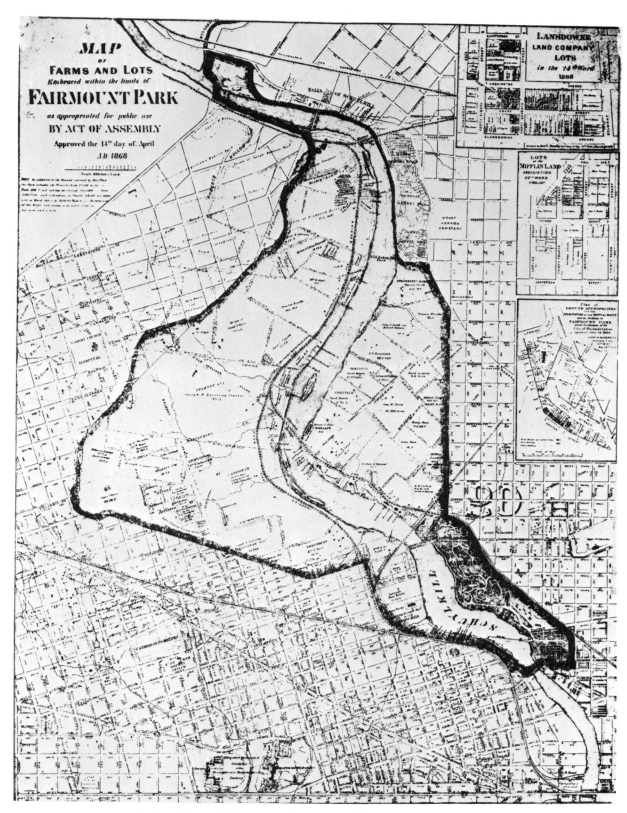

PLATE 3. Map of Fairmount Park as approved by Act of Assembly in 1868.

healthfulness of the banks of the Schuylkill for the inhabitants of the city. For we find that 104 acres of ground to be acquired in 1867 had on both sides of the river "hotels, beer vaults, ice houses, wharves, oil refineries, city and country dwellings, many mills," and lands that had been planned to be five villages of small individual holdings. (Plate 3) This has the sound of events in real estate of a century later; of this we are woefully aware. This land had to be acquired by right of eminent domain authorized by the Act of the Assembly in 1867.

The anxiety of the commission for a pure water supply was further heightened by its estimate that the population of the city would increase in 20 years to a million and a half souls. This estimate was frightfully immature; but then the use of computers was not handy.

Now we come to the first major acquisitions of land to be included in the park. Lemon Hill with its *now* lovely mansion (restored by Dr. Fiske Kimball, late Director of the Philadelphia Art Museum and a resident thereof for many years until his death) was a parcel of 45 acres (Plate 4). It had been the county seat of Robert Morris (the owner of Morris's Folly, a town house designed by Major L'Enfant, designer of Washington's city plan), sold to him together with Sedgley in 1770 by Tench Francis. At the end of the eighteenth century it was purchased by a Mr. Pratt, who gave it the name of Lemon Hill and embellished it so that it became one of the most popular spots of Philadelphia, later to be known as Pratt's Garden. It is believed that this was the first place in America to serve ice cream. Pratt sold it in 1836 for $225,000 to a group who bought it for speculation and probably small-house development. "A commercial revulsion" brought it on the market in 1843 and it was sold to the city for $75,000. The land and the house were allowed to deteriorate until 1855, when an ordinance was passed to "devote [the land] and dedicate to public use, as a Park, the Lemon Hill estate to be known by the name of Fairmount Park." Thus we have the name of the park for the first time.

There was a tract of 34 acres just north of Lemon Hill known as Sedgley that was originally a part of Lemon Hill when owned by Robert Morris. The Sedgley mansion was built in 1799 from designs by Latrobe and was an early example of the Gothic revival in Philadelphia. The house was demolished in 1857. In the same year public subscriptions were secured in the amount of $60,000 and the tract presented to the city subject to a mortgage and dedicated as a part of Fairmount Park. From this time on substantial progress was made by the city "to obtain adequate areas of ground and lay them out and maintain them as open public places for the health and enjoyment of the people forever." Public opinion in Philadelphia was solidly behind this movement, as is illustrated by two members of the family of

PLATE 4. House of Lemon Hill as restored by Dr. Fiske Kimball and lived in until his
death.

Thomas P. Cope who contributed $20,000 and "whose name has been made
honorable in the recollection of Philadelphians by a life of unblemished
purity and excellence."

At a meeting of the commissioners on July 6, 1867, it was directed that
the owners of those lands between the river and the Reading Railroad up to
Columbia bridge from the then Fairmount Park be given notice that their
land, some six properties, would be appropriated for park purposes. At the

same time, inquiries were to be made as to the sale price of properties on each side of the river to Falls Bridge. The commission was reaching out hungrily to preserve both banks for the purity of Schuylkill water.

The special meeting of the commission on July 13, 1867, directed the park police to erect gates at entrances to the park south of Girard Avenue "in keeping with the present fences," and to "cause the gates to be closed at eleven o'clock at night; and to procure and cause to be rung at that hour a bell to warn people to leave."

Jesse George and his sister Rebecca owned farmland of 83 acres on a high hill on the west side of the river. It was exceedingly attractive land and the Georges had refused many offers for it from land speculators who wanted to develop it for residential sites. In 1868 Jesse was 83 years of age and we presume that Rebecca was approximately the same. They deeded their farm to the Park Commission upon their deaths. The commission promptly resolved that it should be known forever as Georges Hill. From the hill the land slopes gradually down to the river and a fine view of the city is to be had from it.

A further Act of Assembly in 1868 directed the commission to appropriate Wissahickon Creek and the shores to the heights on both sides of the creek, such appropriation to include the existing road on the side of the creek (Plate 5). Thus Fairmount Park in 1868 extended from the reservoir "Faire-Mount" to the present Northwestern Avenue or City Line. A report in that year points out that London had 500 acres of parkland for each 100,000 inhabitants and that Phoenix Park in Dublin boasted 1,700 acres and was thought by many to be the finest playground in the world. New York had just put aside 776 acres for Central Park. It would appear, then, that Fairmount Park had become the largest urban park in the world.

In 1867 the park extended on the east side of the river from the reservoir to about the Pennsylvania Railroad (Plate 3). The Act of Assembly of 1868 that officially created the park boundaries included on the east side some 16 additional properties, ranging in size from 12 to 40 acres and extending to Thirty-third Street on the east and to Laurel Hill Cemetery on the north. These properties included, among others, the mansions of Strawberry, Woodford, and Mount Pleasant. On the west side of the river there were some fourteen holdings, ranging in size from about 22 to 140 acres. These included the famous park mansions of Sweetbrier, Lansdowne, Belmont, and Solitude.

In April 1869 the commission ordered that all houses in the park be put into satisfactory condition for rental and that they be "properly and tastefully fitted up." In June of the same year the park engineer was directed to remove the mansion and outbuildings of Egglesfield. I have been unable to find a print showing this house.

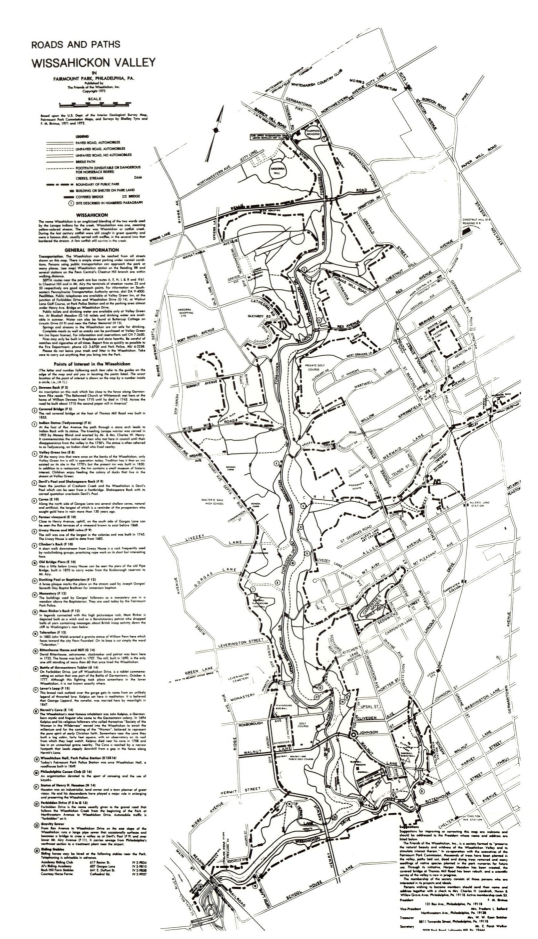

PLATE 5. Contemporary map of the Wissahickon. *Courtesy of Friends of Wissahickon, Inc.*

For some years there had been an active and popular steamboat traffic on the river. This mode of transportation was important to those people living in Manayunk, Germantown, and Roxborough who wanted to enjoy the pleasant excursion to the park. This traffic had become so popular that in 1869 the commission authorized the construction of six landings; these were to be built at Fountain Green, Edgely Point, and Strawberry Mansion on the east bank, and Lansdowne Island, Belmont, and Ford Road on the west bank. At the same time the commission levied a charge of one penny for each person carried by the steamboats, such charge to be returned to the commission.

With the acquisition of land on both banks of the river and the Wissahickon, the commission also acquired many buildings; a large number of these were industrial in character and wholly undesirable from the point of view of rendering the waters fit for consumption in the city. The mansions in the park were, of course, highly desirable, and have been maintained as such. There will be more about these in a later chapter. There is a picturesque quality about the river on warm days in spring and autumn when racing shells are out on the river. The boathouses on the east bank of the river were in existence when the park was formed. However, the commission in October 1867 ordered that those club buildings, built "without regard to architectural adornment," should be replaced by such structures as would be acceptable to the commission by June 1, 1868 (Plate 6). Without pursuing

PLATE 6. Boat House Row on the Schuylkill as it is today.

the history of each boat club, I do not know just how many had to be replaced. Although the line of boat, clubs along the river is quite impressive from the west bank, it can hardly be said that they present a fetching architectural achievement.

One would scarcely recognize the Wissahickon today as the site of a large and important industrial area in the nineteenth century. By the year 1793 there were twenty-four mills, and before the middle of the nineteenth century there were more than sixty. Of the mill factors' houses, only one

PLATE 7.   Wissahickon Hall, an early tavern, now used as a barracks for park police.

exists today–that of David Rittenhouse, who built and operated the first paper mill in the colonies. Until the middle of the nineteenth century the products of these mills reached their markets over rough roads through Germantown.

In 1856 the present road along the creek was completed from Ridge Avenue to City Line in Chestnut Hill by the Wissahickon Turnpike Company. Thus the mill products could be sent to market in Philadelphia and to the towns westward by the Ridge Road. In 1870 the commission ordered that all toll gates along the Wissahickon Turnpike be removed and no further tolls be collected. At the same time the Committee on Plans and Improvement of the commission was "to report whether in their judgement, under all circumstances it is necessary to cause the removal of the Mills now existing along the Wissahickon Creek." As a result of the committee's report, all the mills were torn down, with the one exception of the Megargee Paper Mill near Chestnut Hill, which was allowed to stand until 1884.

There was another group of buildings that reverted to the park in the acquisition of land along the Schuylkill and the Wissahickon–taverns and roadhouses. I have before me a thin volume by Charles S. Keyser, published in 1871, on Fairmount Park. Mr. Keyser was a native of Germantown, and I am told by Mr. John F. Harbeson, who as a young boy played chess with him, that he habitually slept at night on the United States flag. In the back of Mr. Keyser's book are advertisements of the Rock Fish Inn, the Lions at Falls, Wissahickon Hall (Plate 7), and Maple Spring Hotel and Museum (there is no advertisement for Valley Green Inn) (Plate 8). All of these inns and taverns advertise the succulent dish of catfish and waffles; this was indeed the favorite dish along the river and the creek. In fact, Mr. Keyser writes at length of the merits of Schuylkill catfish, alleging them to be vastly superior to the Delaware species of the same fish. But, alas, with the acquisition of these inns and taverns, the commission imposed temperance. It is quite obvious that beer, wine, and whiskey were normal and desirable companions to a platter of catfish and waffles, and when such was denied, the patronage declined to extinction. Today only Wissahickon Hall (a park police barracks) and Valley Green survive as buildings. Belmont Mansion had also become a restaurant in the nineteenth century–but it, too, was a temperance place.

It is evident from the foregoing accounts that the Fairmount Park Commission in the first few years of the establishment of the park were occupied chiefly in the acquisition of land, the maintenance thereof, and the imposition of rules and regulations for the usage of the park. One such regulation is interesting: the commission decreed "that the passage of funeral trains, and of droves of cattle, hogs, sheep and other animals, over Belmont Avenue is prohibited." At the same meeting of the commission in 1871 it

PLATE 8. Valley Green Inn on the Wissahickon, still serving as an eating place.

was stated that "no cattle, sheep or hogs [shall] be driven across bridges between 10 A M and 10 P M and not in greater numbers in other hours of the day than 10 cattle or horses, 20 sheep or hogs—*nor any bull in company with cows"* [my italics] .

In reading the minutes of the meetings of the commission, in faded but beautifully penned script, one wonders that the commission, made up of well-placed Philadelphians, all men of substance and of active business pursuits, could be occupied with what might appear triviality; but these were men who considered their appointments as commissioners with utmost

PLATE 9. Henry Avenue Bridge over the Wissahickon. Paul P. Cret, architect.

PLATE 10.   Trolley bridge over the Schuylkill.

seriousness and held the park in high regard in the social life of the city. In the early years they met every six to ten days, and the absentee was rare. The Honorable Morton McMichael, former mayor of Philadelphia, was for many years president of the commission, and it seems to me quite proper that his statue is in Fairmount Park. Indeed, he advised the commission in June 1869 that he "contemplated" visiting Europe. The commissioners promptly authorized him to visit foreign parks and "to represent this Commission in visiting such foreign parks, and in soliciting and obtaining such information with reference to their laying out and adornment and their

PLATE 11.   Terrace of the Waterworks (see frontispiece). Possibly by Robert Mills with Frederick Graff.

government and administration." This, I am sure, he did with his usual care, sense of responsibility, and devotion to Fairmount Park.

From the very earliest days of the park, the commission from time to time appropriated funds for planting within the park. A typical entry in the minutes of the commission reads thus:

1. For plowing and seeding $5,000.
2. For gardening   5,000.
3. For care of nurseries   2,000.
4. For purchase of tools   3,000.
5. The gardener is "authorized
   to cause plants and evergreens
   to be purchased from the Nurseries
   of Mr. Lingsem of Hackensack,
   New Jersey for $2,500."

And occasionally there would be authorization for the park engineer to purchase another yoke of oxen.

I have before me the annual report of the commission for the year 1878, which gives in many pages a detailed and named account of the many species of shrubs and trees in the park, together with their number and value. It also details those plants which were gifts to the park. This part of the report was undoubtedly the work of John Rennie, who was appointed chief gardener in January 1871 at a salary of $1,500 per year. He notes that the "valuable collection now contains 590 species and 450 varieties of deciduous and evergreen trees and shrubs. An arboretum which compares favorably with any in this country or abroad." Rennie had been encouraged in his work and his learning, for the commission had appropriated $150 for books on horticulture as the beginning of a library on such subjects.

The same annual report contains reference to the "Plantarium," a nursery or stock ground of some 20 acres in which there were 30,000 trees and shrubs of evergreen and deciduous quality. From this, in the years 1866 and 1867, the value of trees and shrubs planted in the park was $14,490. The trees added in the preceding year were 1,532 and those purchased amounted to 1,243, while the number taken from the stock was 9,672. There were 34 presentations of assorted plants from sympathetic nurseries or individuals in 1877 with the monetary value of $5,550.

The Botanic Garden was established in 1877 between Horticultural Hall on the east, Georges Hill on the west, Lansdowne Valley on the south, and Belmont Valley on the north. This garden was the result of a request by the Pennsylvania Horticultural Society "for the formation of an Arboretum, the object of which is to exhibit a classified collection of plants for the improvement of botanical science, including living specimens of such as are

PLATE 12. Gate on East River Drive attributed to Frank Furness, architect. It was moved from the Centennial grounds.

PLATE 13. Detail of the Undine Club boathouse on the Schuylkill. Furness and Evans, architects.

useful in medicine . . . for the acclimation of foreign plants, with a view to their dissemination over the country."

I cannot leave these historical remarks on horticulture in the park without mention of Horticultural Hall, designed by Schwarzmann for the Centennial. It was one of the most remarkable buildings of its kind in this country and was demolished within my memory. In fact, I attended its demolition at eight o'clock on the first morning of that sad occasion and shed an architectural tear over its demise. It was divided into four "Houses":

1. Economic House—medicinal and food plants: 100 species.
2. Forcing House—hothouse plants and plants for forcing.
3. Temperate House—half hardy plants and a collection of Australian plants.
4. Fernery House—100 species and 23 species of mosses.

Eighty thousand plants were propagated in the year of the Centennial.

Now we come to two very substantial gifts to the horticulture of the park. François André Michaux, botanist to the king of France, "who travelled long in this country, and described our oaks and finest trees in a work of great merit and splendor," bequeathed at his death $6,000 to the American Philosophical Society. The society proposed that the legacy be expended in Fairmount Park "as a memorial to him and his father of their devotion and to promote the objects which had occupied their lives." Michaux had identified forty species of oaks in North America. The society stipulated that a grove of oaks to be named "Michaux Grove" be established in the park, which should grow at least two oaks of "every kind that will endure in this climate." Any surplus of the fund was to be spent cultivating two kinds of oaks for distribution to public parks in the country. The commission further authorized $500 for oaks to be imported from foreign nurseries for the grove. This grove is located on both sides of Lansdowne Drive, beginning at Belmont Avenue and extending to the west end of the site of Horticultural Hall. It contains 44 species of oaks.

Elliot Cresson left a legacy to the park for planting. The minutes of the commission read: "to cause a portion of the income of [his] legacy to be expended in shade trees in the Park in a situation to protect the citizens from the sun . . . [to be called] the Cresson Grove, excluding therefrom lombardy poplars, ailanthus, poplar, mulberry and similar exotics as his will requires." I do not know where this grove is located.

It is quite clear from reading the minutes of the commission and other sources of research on the park that, although the park was established primarily for the protection of the city's water supply, the citizens of Philadelphia quickly came to the realization that they possessed a park that was truly unique. They were (and still are) proud of it and jealously

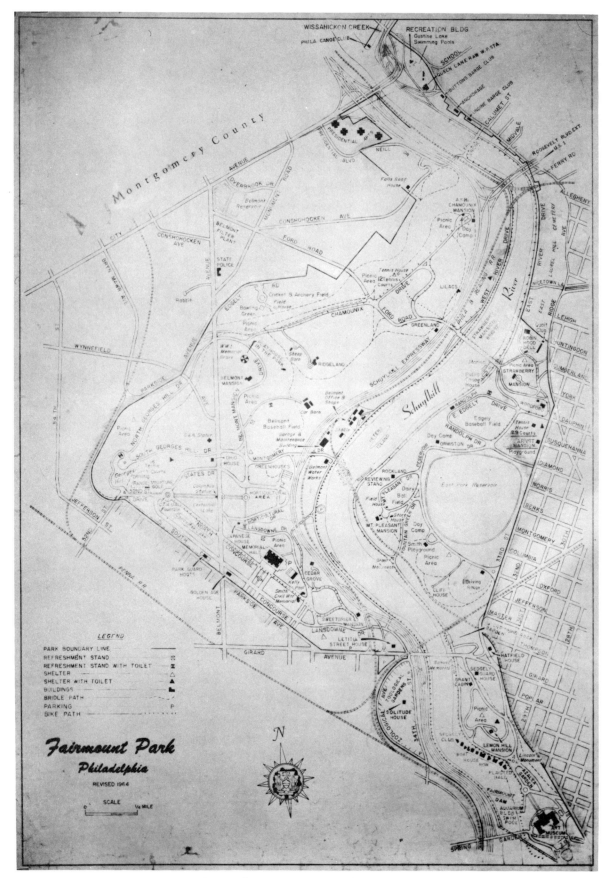

PLATE 14. Contemporary map of Fairmount Park.

regarded it as a sanctuary. The forced removal of all industrial and utilitarian structures from the banks of the Schuylkill and the Wissahickon opened vast spaces of extremely pleasant views and ground that *nature* had designed for a marvelous park. There had been no formal designing of the park by architects and, indeed, it was not necessary. The minutes of the commission reveal that roads and paths were laid out with the utmost informality, with the result that one can readily find oneself lost in the park. This is part of its charm.

2

Frederick Law Olmsted Reports

There are those in Philadelphia who contend that the justly famous and able landscape architect, Frederick Law Olmsted, designed or contributed largely to the plan of Fairmount Park. I can find no record or justification for this assertion. It is to the credit and taste of the commissioners that they did invite him on two occasions to come to Philadelphia to consult with them concerning the broad aspects of the park or, as recorded, "for a cursory view and general consultation." For this first trip in 1867 he was paid his requested fee of $200.

It was indeed a modest fee considering the reputation he had achieved in designing New York's Central Park of some 770 acres, including 150 acres of water reservoirs.

Olmsted (Plate 15) became a professional landscape architect strictly by osmosis. He intended to enter Yale, but his real interest was farming. An indulgent father set him up in farming, first in Connecticut (which failed) and finally in Staten Island. But Olmsted was also a wanderer. He left his farm at those times when a really serious agriculturist was most needed on his land. He traveled extensively in the southern states, acquiring a distaste for them and their condition. There was a trip to England, again at the wrong time of the agricultural year for a farmer, ostensibly to study English horticulture.

PLATE 15. Frederick Law Olmsted, circa 1860. *Courtesy of Olmsted Associates, Brookline, Mass.*

But the city lured him. He wrote rather extensively and very well. In 1852 he published *Walks and Talks of an American Farmer in England* and a few years later made an effort at magazine publishing. This was an unfortunate venture and failed.

By one of those quirks in a man's career, he applied for and received the position of superintendent of Central Park in New York. This was in 1857. His biographer, Silvia Sutton, remarks that "by April of the following year, he had become a landscape architect." One must admit that the transition from "gentleman farmer," writer, and magazine publisher to landscape architect in less than two years is indeed remarkable. A contemporary landscape architect with the required seven years of university training would shudder at the statement.

Olmsted's sole training, if the term may be used, in landscaping was the practice of agronomy and his observations of English gardens and parks. These distinctions must have been impressive, since Calvert Vaux invited him as associate in creating a design for Central Park. Vaux was an English architect who had been persuaded by Andrew Jackson Downing (that arbiter of taste in architecture and landscaping in Victorian America) to come to this country in 1850. It was Downing who gave Vaux his knowledge of landscape architecture. Vaux was a young man and, as did so many young men then, and indeed today, he entered an open competition for Central Park with Olmsted, working nights and weekends against thirty-two competitors. They won, and Olmsted was appointed chief architect for the park. Out of the competition came the firm of Olmsted and Vaux, which lasted until 1872.

I do not know the physical or topographical condition of the 770 acres of Central Park when New York City set it aside for a park; but since the park took twenty-five years to complete this would indicate that it was largely unfinished ground. Such a condition was in striking contrast to Fairmount Park. However, in each instance the park was on the outer edge of the thickly populated areas, but in both cities the municipal authorities cannily foresaw the rapid expansion of the two cities to the north, east, and west in the very near future.

The result of this foresight was the ultimate location of splendid parks in the approximate center of each of the metropolises, with reasonable public access from all directions. This is very different from former locating of public parks in most American cities. Generally, such parks were made on land on the periphery of the city and on ground that was swampy and of no practical use for commercial or residentail utilization. Olmsted's biographer states that the development of Central Park was an inspiration to other cities. This fact can hardly be subject to doubt, for the urbanization of

America was coming into its own and demanding the physically social amenities such as well-planned and well-located public parks. Fairmount Park could hardly offer the same kind of inspiration, for it was already a "natural" park in contrast to the "made" park of Central Park.

Nevertheless, the commissioners of Fairmount Park were prominent, were truly "City Fathers," and were seeking expert and cultivated advice and direction. In this they were approached by Robert Copeland of Boston, who described himself as "landscape gardener" and requested the appointment as architect for the "extensive Park." It is not in the record that Copeland ever came on to have a look at Fairmount Park nor that the park commission traveled to examine any of his work as it did to see Olmsted's in New York and Brooklyn. Copeland's proposal to the commission was short and did not mention fees, but contained this distinctive paragraph:

> If this is to be a penurious affair or if I am to be subject to the control in matters of taste of those whom I did not think my equals in such matters I should not care to undertake it.

Mr. Copeland did not understnad that one did not talk to Philadelphians in such a manner.

Olmsted had resigned five times as architect for Central Park because of tasteless and tactless treatment from politicians and such. In fact, he traveled constantly from Brooklyn across the country to Berkeley, California, and was badgered and frustrated in his many projects by people of poor taste and worse appreciation; but then, he was an idealist and as such expected and suffered the slurs of the ignorant.

Copeland continued in his letter that he had "made plans" for over 200 country places and 15 cemeteries. He pointed out that he had submitted two plans in the Central Park competition and had been assured "by all the competitors I met including Mr. Olmsted that I should receive first prize." This would appear to be a question of who was kidding whom.

Olmsted had originally proposed two trips to Fairmount Park for consultation with the commission. He came on again in November 1867 for the purpose of discussing the boundaries of the park. He had quoted a fee of $500 for his trip but was paid $748. I cannot account for the difference. His report to the commission is carefully recorded in the bound records of the park in the graceful, flowing script (now quite faded) of the secretary to the board. It covers fifteen pages approximately ten by fourteen inches, and is the epitome of completeness.

Olmsted found that a well-matured and liberal scheme had grown up for laying out a "public pleasure ground, for protecting the purity of the water supply of the city and for controlling the shores of the Schuylkill between

Fairmount Dam and the Wissahickon Creek" or Ridge Avenue.

I shall quote rather extensively from his report, for the recommendations he made over a hundred years ago were generally included—with one major exception—in the Fairmount Park we know today.

The following quotation would seem to be Olmsted's definition, and indeed an absolute requirement, for a "public pleasure ground."

> Such a [comprehensive Park] scheme should in the first place provide ample opportunity for comparatively private walking exercise in fresh air; it should also include liberal provision for driving and riding unhampered by obstructions that occur in city streets; its next and in many respects its most important object should be to appropriate the best view of beautiful landscape pictures that can be included within a tract of ground of not unreasonable extent; and its last main purpose . . . should be to secure ground which while rural, delicate and refined in general character and abounding in suggestions at least of seclusion and tranquility should also be recognized as offering an opportunity and occasion for constantly receiving public gatherings of a lively and festive character.

By today's standards we would call Olmsted a socialist, a humanitarian, a lover of people, and a planner for the comforts and delight of people without regard to economic or social status. This is a theme that recurs all through his writings. He was a Walt Whitman in city planning, and in this vein he continues:

> It may be considered one of the great advantages of a public domain of this kind that it gives occasion for the coming together of the poor and the rich on the ground which is common possession and that it produces a feeling which to the poor is a relief from the sense of restriction, which they generally experience elsewhere in comparing their limits of activity with the apparent freedom of those whose cares and duties have a wider scope. As art deals with the manners and morals of men through the imagination; this is one of the many reasons why the expression of amplitude and free sweep in the scenery of a park which can only be produced by broad meadow-like surfaces with shadowy and uncertain limits, is an artistic requirement of the first importance.

For instance, in the "broad meadow-like surfaces," he mentions Georges Hill and states "that the land between it and the river is the most important which it will be in your power to enclose for Park purposes." Another such "meadow-like" surface is the view from Belmont, and although he concedes that it is worth inclusion in the park, he devotes but one sentence to its merits. The appeal of Georges Hill is the long slope of meadow down to the river, which at that point is "still," and that of the opposite bank leading up to a gentle level of hills.

He discusses the approaches to the park at some length. He points out that, since the main and thickly settled part of the city is to the east of the park, the approach from that direction becomes extremely important. He suggests that Thirty-fifth Street (I really think he meant Thirty-fourth Street) would be an excellent approach, connecting the new South Street, Market, and Chestnut Street bridges and thence across the Wire Bridge into the Park. This would give a western access to that part of the park east of the Schuylkill, while a continuance of Thirty-fourth Street would provide a direct entrance to the park west of the river.

Of course, the Wire Bridge no longer exists. It was at the foot of Fairmount in approximately the location of the present Spring Garden Street bridge. It was a most important crossing of the river. It was a suspension bridge designed by Col. Charles Ellet, Jr., and is justly claimed to be the first wire suspension bridge in America. It measured 343 feet between the stone abutments and was really a rather picturesque structure.

It is indeed fortunate that Olmsted's recommendation for using Thirty-fifth Street as an entrance to the park was not adopted. Although the Zoological Garden had been incorporated in 1859, very little by way of building, if any, had been accomplished by the time of his report. The use of Thirty-fifth Street would have cut through the present zoo grounds and virtually destroyed it as a site for the zoo, since its total of forty acres is limited in extent by Thirty-fourth Street (the river) and the Pennsylvania Railroad. Doubtless he envisaged another long sweep of meadow from Thirty-fifth Street down to the river. How fortunate for his aesthetic sensibilities that he could not foresee the desecration of the Expressway in its brutal path through the park. I am reminded of John B. Kelley's famous remark when he was chairman of the commission, "Thank God, my grandchildren will never be able to say that I approved the Expressway going through the Park."

Since the most populous part of the city was east of the river and the park, he suggested that Spring Garden Street be widened and "distinguished as the [principal] approach to Fairmount Park." This would, of course, provide a monumental gateway from the congested part of the city. Considering that the Benjamin Franklin Parkway was not even a dream as a means of access, it was a brilliant suggestion, and because of the Wire Bridge it gave convenient entrance to the area west of the river.

Olmsted was not unaware of the possible and probable expansion of the congested eastern part of the city and of that part to the west of the river, nor were the commissioners. A very great portion of what is now known as West Fairmount Park, lying west of the river and much better than a mile in depth, was composed of large farming estates; some were as much as two hundred acres in area. Beyond that, the map of 1868 shows West Philadelphia laid out in a gridiron pattern much like Thomas Holme's map of 1682, for the area between the Delaware and the Schuylkill rivers. But it is doubtful if it was extensively populated. Thus West Philadelphia had easy access to the park without the necessity of broad avenues, for that area consisted of large estates and farms that were quickly acquired as park land. Because of the natural division of the city into two areas, Olmsted refers to the park as a "buffer zone." This, in truth, is precisely what it is, and those of us who habitually travel from the two areas of the city find that it forms a pleasant and beautiful relief from the monotony of a modern metropolis.

He further predicted that the area west of the park would became "semi-rural and suburban in character. Such an improvement adequately developed would probably *without expense to the City* add materially to its attractiveness as a place of residence and it would certainly offer a very agreeable adjunct to the facilities for pleasure travel to be provided within the Park itself."

He looked even further for an extension of the park, and the Wissahickon Creek area obviously came to his inventive and naturalist eye. He pointed out that what we know as Wissahickon Drive, some seven miles long, was a natural road extension of the East Park Road. In his own words: "the Creek [Wissahickon] Road offers such unparalleled attractions for driving, it is so accessible and convenient of approach and can be secured at this time at a cost so moderate, that no route can at all be compared it."

By Act of Assembly in 1868, the commission was directed to appropriate the Wissahickon and its shores to the heights on either side of the creek and to include the road on the side of the creek.

I have no authority for this statement, but I suspect that Olmsted probably said to the commission, over food and drink in a congenial place and in rather frank conversation after his two trips to Fairmount Park, that he could offer no radical or planned suggestions in a park wrought by nature. It was one of those wonderful places possessing woods, streams, and natural convolutions of terrain. Landscape architecture, generally considered, is the planning of man. But in Fairmount Park the fact of a major river and a fast-flowing creek merged into landscape entity; moreover, bounded by rocky hills and in the almost precise center of the most important city in the eastern part of the country, it was the architectural dream of the landscapist.

After all, Olmsted, in New York's Central Park, had been and was professionally dealing with a relatively flat plateau (a few boulders and some water) in a metropolis, where the threat of human and architectural congestion had already been made evident—and moreover promised a great deal more of the same. He had planned and worked on most difficult sites in addition to Central Park, in Brooklyn, Boston (one of his less admired ones), and in Berkeley, California.

I should have thought that over his whiskey he might have said, "Gentlemen, you have a park—God-given; make the most of it and plant a lot of trees." This they did, as I have stated in an earlier part of this book.

I have on the walls of my study a plan of Fairmount Park, drawn the year Olmsted was consulted and made by an unsigned engineer, entitled *Maps of Farms and Lots embraced within the limits of Fairmount Park — By Act of Assembly — 14th day of April* A.D. *1868.* Next to it is a drawing covering the same limits of the park made from contemporary documents by the architectural office of Hatfield, Martin and White, dated 1964. There is no substantial difference; in fact, the two are almost identical.

Olmsted seems to me to have been one of the great men of his century, because he had the innate perspicacity to refrain from messing up something that begged to be left in its natural state.

But the commission was not quite through with Olmsted. In December 1869 the Committee on Plans and Improvements was authorized to confer with Olmsted and Vaux, "Landscape gardeners and architects," for the "preparation of a plan for the permanent laying out and improvement of the Park" and to ascertain the terms for such work. The vote was 6 to 5 for the resolution—hardly a smashing vote of confidence.

In January 1871 Olmsted and Vaux, "Landscape artists and Gardeners," were authorized to plan for the "permanent improvement of so much of Fairmount Park, as lies East of the Schuylkill River—the compensation to be paid for their services not to exceed $15 per acre." This was their usual fee. Consequent to this they presented a plan together with a report in August 1871; this was "laid on the table."

It appears that, coincident with the preparation of the Olmsted-Vaux plan for the east or "old" park, H. J. Schwarzmann, "senior engineer" for the park, was also engaged in making a plan for the same part of the park. There is no record that he had been instructed by the commission to prepare such a plan. However, both plans came up for consideration by the commission on January 25, 1872, and the Schwarzmann plan was adopted.

I have searched for these plans in many places from Boston to Washington, without success. Consequently, I am unable to describe the Schwarzmann plan. In fact, it is quite possible that the plan was not put into effect.

This was the end of Frederick Law Olmsted's connection with Fairmount Park.

3

The Zoo

A local newspaper commented in 1867:

There is in our city, unfortunately, a great dearth of healthy forms of amusement offered to the public, and in looking over the statistics of European cities, we find that gardens of this kind [Zoos] have greater attention paid to them than any other places of recreation. A collection of our own animals would form a noble addition to our Park. In fact our western prairies and mountains are filled with animals which we feel safe in saying have only been seen by Indians and hardy trappers. Our idea of foreign animals is based upon the half-starved and cowed brutes which are dragged around the country in wagons, and which in a short time, so lose every vestige of their natural habits, that as studies of natural history they are utterly valueless. Then again, the establishments where they are exhibited are of such a character that they are the last places we would wish our young people to frequent. In London, the Zoological Society's Gardens are filled with children from morning to night.

Six years later the Board of Managers of the Zoological Society of Philadelphia read into the first annual report:

44

The Board is desirous that the scientific purposes of the Society shall be carefully regarded, and hopes much from the influences which the Garden will exert in fostering a love for such pursuits, and promoting the health and education of all classes. An opportunity will be presented for gathering together men of various tastes, who may assist in contributing their knowledge and ability to inform and delight the entire community. The many whose occupations or necessities compel them to remain in the city during the summers, will derive physical and mental benefit from the Zoological Garden, and will cause it to be highly prized and affectionately regarded.

Neither the editors of the newspaper in 1867 nor the board of managers in 1873 could foresee that in the first few years of the Philadelphia Zoo the most comfortable and pleasant means of visiting it would be by steamboat on the Schuylkill to the wharf at the zoo, or that one of the truly exciting animals would be the gift of Mrs. William Tecumseh Sherman of the cow "Atlanta," which had accompanied her famous husband on his famous "March to the Sea" through Georgia. I know of another zoo that can only be approached by boat and that is in the harbor of Helsinki in Finland. There one boards a small but comfortable ferry at quayside and disembarks on an island devoted exclusively to a small but charming zoo and the residence of the director. If one is fortunate in having a letter to the director, the visitor receives a personally conducted tour of the island by him and afterwards sherry in his house with his lovely wife.

The nineteenth-century European or American zoo was no new accomplishment among civilized people. Dr. William Biddle Cadwalader, an engaging president of the Philadelphia Zoo, noted in a paper read before the Newcomen Society of America in 1929, that the earliest zoological gardens for which there is a definite record were established by the first emperor of the Chou Dynasty in China about a thousand years before Christ. It was known as "Intelligence Park," which implied an educational purpose. Moreover, Cadwalader stated, "Under Ptolemy II, as part of the festival of Dionysus, a great procession through the stadium of the City of Alexandria was said to have taken *all day*. A remarkable assemblage of animals formed a part of this parade — elephants and groups of other animals in harness drawing chariots, camels laden with spices, sheep, oxen, bears, leopards, lions, and birds in cages were included. Twenty-four hundred hounds also passed in review and there were a hundred and fifty men carrying trees to which were attached animals and birds of all sorts."*

*George Jennison, ANIMALS FOR SHOW AND PLEASURE IN ANCIENT ROME (Manchester, England: Manchester University Press, 1937).

It was William Camac, M.D., graduate of Jefferson Medical College, who was the enthusiastic promoter of the Zoological Society of Philadelphia. He had traveled widely abroad and had had many opportunities to visit zoological gardens. In 1859 he called together at his house several men to discuss means of establishing a zoo in Philadelphia. Among these were John Leconte, M.D., one of the nation's most outstanding naturalists, and John Cassin, the best known ornithologist of his time. Others were described as "financially solid and distinguished citizens." In the beginning there were thirty-six members and incorporators of the society, the charter for which was granted in the same year. Dr. Camac was elected president.

Two years later the Civil War broke out and distracted attention from the embryonic zoo. In March of 1872 the members met for reorganization, again in Dr. Camac's house, with William and John Merrick, John Ridgeway, and Fairman Rogers. Dr. Camac was reelected president. A committee was appointed to wait on the commissioners of Fairmount Park for the purpose of selecting a site for the zoo. The commissioners assigned a long and narrow strip of five acres just below the Lincoln Statue on the present East River Drive. Fortunately, this site was abandoned before any construction took place. Another site was offered by the commissioners in the East Park above Girard Avenue Bridge and this too was abandoned. Finally, the present site at the western end of the bridge was settled upon, containing the John Penn mansion, Solitude, and its grounds, amounting to some thirty-three acres.

A sizable portion of this site was unusable by the zoo, since a temporary railroad ran through it carrying materials for the construction of the Girard Avenue Bridge. However, in 1873 a high fence was erected around ten or eleven acres, including the mansion Solitude. Thus came about the beginning of the first zoo in America.

Now events in the establishment of the zoo happened rapidly. After the Civil War people traveled extensively in Europe and England and consequently became acquainted with foreign zoological gardens, most especially the London Garden in Regent's Park, founded in 1828 and probably the prototype of the modern zoo. This indubitably led to a better understanding of the place of a zoological garden in the Philadelphia community.

The first and most important consideration in the implementation of the acquisition of a permanent site was the question of financing the zoo. The society's by-laws were completely "remodeled," so that additional capital funds could be obtained. This was accomplished by loan certificates of stock of one hundred dollars to bear an interest rate of six percent and, curiously, an additional interest of two and one-half percent in the form of tickets to the zoo. The stock was quickly subscribed by public-spirited citizens to the amount of $320,000. In later years the greater part of this loan was

PLATE 16. Solitude in the zoo. This was the house of John Penn. Until recently it served as the administration building of the zoo.

voluntarily surrendered to the society. Philadelphians are always generous in supporting a cause that adds to the cultural life of the city.

At this time H. J. Schwarzmann, engineer for the Fairmount Park Commission, who very likely was already engaged in the preliminary studies for Memorial Hall and Horticultural Hall for the Centennial Exhibition, was commissioned not only to lay out paths, location, and size of buildings and planting for the new zoo, but to travel abroad, visiting zoological gardens and examining buildings and methods of exhibiting animals and birds.

PLATE 17.   Veranda of Solitude overlooking the Schuylkill.

With money in the till, the board of managers (now referred to as directors) turned to construction of buildings. John Vaughan Merrick was appointed chairman of the Committee on Construction. In his memoirs he notes that in the incredibly short time of two years the following buildings were constructed: the north entrance (Plate 18), the Monkey House (Plate 19) (later rebuilt as a Reptile House), the Reptile House (later becoming the Aviary) (Plate 20), these by Theophilus P. Chandler, architect; the Elephant House (Plate 21), Furness and Hewitt, architects; the Deer House (Plates 22,

PLATE 18.   North gate of zoo. Furness and Hewitt, architects, 1875.

PLATE 19. Monkey House in the zoo. Theophilus P. Chandler, architect.

PLATE 20.   Bird House in the zoo. Mellor and Meigs, architects. Completely new interior by Bolton, Martin and White, architects.

PLATE 21.   Pachyderm House in the zoo. Paul P. Cret, architect.

PLATE 22.   Antelope House in the zoo. George W. Hewitt, architect, 1877.

23), Hewitt, architect; Lion House, Collins and Autenrieth, architects; and the Sea Lions Pool, Eagle House, and Deer Enclosures.

John Merrick later encountered opposition from the board in his selection of architects (a not-uncommon occurrence) and as a result resigned as chairman of his committee but remained on the board and became vice-president in 1886.

Now that the zoo had buildings, a lake, and a fresh-flowing stream, it was time to procure animals and birds. This process was greatly simplified by

PLATE 23.   Interior of Antelope House.

general public interest as well as that of the government in Washington. In an early report noted in the minutes of the board of managers, it is stated:

> It is the aim of the Managers, not only to afford the public an agreeable resort for rational recreation, but by the extent of their [the Zoo] collection, to furnish the *greatest facilities for scientific observation.* (My italics). So far as their means allow, they are on the alert to procure all desirable specimens of animated nature. The great interest which the Society has inspired in Philadelphia and abroad, in merchants owning vessels trading in foreign ports, and especially taken by the Smithsonian Institution, the President and Secretaries of War and Navy, who have with great kindness, issued circular letters in behalf of the Society of their officers, has greatly enlarged our means of acquisition and leads us to believe that, at no distant date, our collection will rival those of the most famous gardens of Europe.

Frank J. Thompson, an extraordinary man and an experienced collector of animals, then in Australia, was engaged by cable as the first superintendent of the zoo and authorized to purchase animals. In his remarkable career he had been in Africa and camped at the falls of Zambesi before Stanley or Livingston. He had dug diamonds in Kimberly, South Africa, before the British monopolized the mines. A London newspaper commented on the appointment: "Mr. Thompson has been for many years a naturalist and natural history collector, not merely in South Africa [he was then in Capetown], but most parts of the world; and of him, more than of most men, we might say he is to the manner born— a perfect enthusiast in his profession."

It is not surprising, then, that when the Zoological Garden opened on July 1, 1874, there were 282 animals on exhibit, 674 birds, 50 monkeys, and 8 reptiles. Represented were antelopes, lions, zebras, kangaroos, an elephant, a rhinoceros, and a tiger. There had been numerous offers of animals and Theodore L. Harrison had contributed a fine collection of more than one hundred cages of birds.

General James S. Brisbin, United States Army, was stationed at Omaha, Nebraska. In 1873 he was requested and authorized to purchase animals from the western plains. This he did gratuitously, probably from a keen interest in animals and America's first zoo. In the one year the zoo received from him grizzly, black, cinnamon, and brown bears (Plate 24), two silver foxes, moose, elk, wildcats, wolverines, eagles, and black-tailed doe.

Brigham Young, of the Mormon Church, sent on two bears. Mrs. Sherman, wife of the general, presented "Atlanta," the cow that had followed the General in his march in Georgia and taken part in the triumphal parade in

PLATE 24. Bear pits in the zoo. Theophilus P. Chandler, architect. This is one of the very early exhibits in the zoo.

Washington after the war, with the pious hope that in the zoo "she might pass the remainder of her life in peace." Indeed, she deserved peace, for her existence with General Sherman in Georgia must have been rather rough, and she might well have agreed with her owner that "war is hell."

The acquisition and transporting of animals by General Brisbin or Frank Thompson was not a simple procedure. Railroad lines did indeed cross this country, but there were vast stretches that were isolated from the new railroads. However, the railroads were interested in the new zoo and allowed animals from the West free transportation to Philadelphia. Animals coming from foreign countries were not exempt from a customs fee until Congress passed a bill allowing free entry for all animals consigned to the Philadelphia Zoo.

The year 1874 saw the completion of the Girard Avenue Bridge and the destruction of the Wire Bridge. Thus the only land access from the city to the zoo was from Girard Avenue. This was not an easy way for people in Germantown, Roxborough, and Manayunk, nor, indeed, was it easy for those people in center city. I have noted that there was an active and frequent steamboat service on the Schuylkill and, to take advantage of this, a wharf was built near the western end of the Girard Avenue Bridge, which meant only a short walk to the north entrance of the zoo.

During the first eight months of the zoo there were 227,557 visitors, and the society's membership was in excess of 600 members. In 1867, the Centennial year, the zoo hosted 677,630, a record that has been met and exceeded only within the last few years. Now, weather permitting, it is not uncommon to have over a million visitors in a year. At this writing the membership of the society numbers 4,858.

But we come to another Philadelphia first (there are so many of them), that is, the establishment of a research and pathological laboratory in the zoo, the first one in this country. This had its beginnings in 1874 when Henry Cadwalader Chapman, M.D., Sc.D., Jefferson Medical College, was appointed prosector (one who makes dissections) to the society. This was the year after he thanked the managers of the society for the opportunity to personally dissect a specimen of the Musang,* the results of which he reported orally to a meeting of the Academy of Natural Sciences. As prosector he was able to supply many published contributions in the Proceedings of the Academy; among these papers were discourses on the anatomy of the monkey, the giraffe, the elephant, and other animals. He also reported that his observation of the zoo led him to believe that the deaths of animals in the first six months of the operation of the zoo were caused largely by improper food, badly regulated temperature, and ill-designed cages. He became a director of the zoo in 1881 and served as secretary to the board for several years.

Although the work of Dr. Chapman in dissection was probably "the pursuit of knowledge for its own sake," according to Dr. Cadwalader, it soon became obvious that the knowledge gained thereby had a very practical

*Palm-Civet: common name, Toddy-cat. Discovered in 1821.

effects on the life span of animals in captivity. This was recognized by Charles B. Penrose, M.D., at one time president of the society, and in 1905 he established the research laboratory so that scientific results of pathological studies of animals could be systematically recorded and practically applied. The laboratory is now known as the Penrose Research Laboratory in honor of Dr. Penrose. Cortland Y. White, M.D., of the University of Pennsylvania, was the first director of the laboratory, in addition to his activities in the hospital of the university.

Dr. White was succeeded by Herbert L. Fox, M.D., also of the University of Pennsylvania. In 1923 Dr. Fox published an unusual volume, *Disease in Captive Wild Mammals and Birds,* which was a résumé of the work of the laboratory to that time. "Heretofore, no such thorough presentation of this original and rather obscure subject had appeared in the literature of comparative medical sciences." This again is according to Dr. Cadwalader.

It was discovered in the laboratory that primates were particularly susceptible to tuberculosis. A method of applying a tuberculin test to these animals was worked out and no primate was admitted to the collection without such a test being applied. It was also found that this disease could be transferred from the human spectator to the primate and consequently all cages containing these animals were equipped in front with glass partitions. Due to these preventive measures, the first chimpanzee and orangutan born in captivity in this country occurred at the Philadelphia Zoo. Since then, the birth of these animals has become somewhat commonplace at the zoo.

Quite early in its functioning the laboratory attracted the attention of federal health agencies. As a result grants were forthcoming from these governmental agencies for research and, indeed, for enlarging the laboratory building. Such a grant was made in the sum of $500,000 by the National Institute of Health for a study over a five-year period of the genetics of salt-induced high blood pressure. In addition, the staff of the laboratory cooperated in research studies with Philadelphia hospitals such as the University of Pennsylvania, the Children's Hospital, and the Cancer Institute in Fox Chase. The various directors of the laboratory have all had a common aim: the prevention of disease in the zoo collection, since it was recognized that treatment of disease was rarely satisfactory.

The renaissance of the zoo began in 1938 when Dr. Cadwalader was president and it continued steadily under presidents Radcliffe Cheston, Jr., George F. Tyler, Jr., and John Williams. The first children's zoo in the world was opened in 1938. This contained domestic animals only, and was replaced in 1957 with the present children's zoo, which mostly houses wild animals. Martin and White were the architects. Also in 1938 the Service Building was constructed, and the Elephant House (Plate 21) opened in 1941. World War

PLATE 25. Rare Mammal House in the zoo. Harbeson, Hough, Livingston and Larson, architects.

II interrupted the building program, but this was continued with the Bird House in 1951 (Plate 20), and in the next year a new Lion House was constructed. The Rare Mammal House (Plate 25) was built in 1965 and the Carnivora House in 1951. The Small Mammal House (Plate 26) opened in 1967, and the Wolf Woods were completed and opened in 1973.

The Elinor S. Gray Memorial Hummingbird Exhibit was built in 1970 with funds privately donated, and a new administration building was constructed to replace the Penn Mansion, Solitude. The African Plains section is presently being completed.

PLATE 26. Small Mammal House in the zoo. Hatfield, Martin and White, architects.

The zoo has been most fortunate in being the recipient of private donations by many individuals who were devoted to the institution and who recognized its place in the environment of the city as a recreational and scientific necessity. These funds came in large part from Mr. Wilson Catherwood and the Dietrich Foundation and its president, Mr. Richard Dietrich. The Hummingbird House and the Wolf Woods were financed by private donations. Great credit must be given to the city for its generosity in steadily, each year, appropriating money for the expansion of the zoo.

I cannot end this chapter without fond mention of the Impala Fountain. Mrs. Herbert C. Morris donated the funds to erect the fountain in memory of her husband, who had served for many years as treasurer and vice-president of the zoo board. Henry Mitchell was the sculptor of the dozen or so animals in the fountain and supervised its casting in bronze in Milan, Italy. Hatfield, Martin and White, architects, collaborated with him in the design of the plaza and the pool. It is one of the really large fountains in Philadelphia and a source of great interest to children.

The Philadelphia Zoo is in many ways unique. It is one of the smallest zoos among the major zoos in the world — barely forty acres; but it is famous. Every zoo keeper in the world knows it and is ecstatic about its collection (after all Freeman Shelly, its director for thirty years in its renaissance, was president of the International Union of Directors of Zoological Gardens). I have been in many zoos in this country and abroad and can report that one has only to mention an architectural connection with the Philadelphia Zoo to receive a warm welcome and the red-carpet treatment.

Philadelphia has achieved a marvelous first in establishing the first zoo in America.

4

The Centennial Year of 1876

Memorial Hall is the last major building remaining from the Centennial Exhibition. It was designed as an art museum and served as such during the Centennial and for many years thereafter, until the collection was either absorbed in the Philadelphia Museum of Art or was sold. For some years it was vacant and badly cared for. Then in 1957 the city retained the architectural firm of Hatfield, Martin, and White to restore the building and put it to modern use by the Fairmount Park Commission. In a lengthy illustrated report to the commission, the architects included a preface in which Dr. George B. Tatum discussed certain aspects of the Centennial as background for "The Adaptation of Memorial Hall." Together with his students, Dr. Tatum, then of the University of Pennsylvania (presently of the University of Delaware), had done some research on the Centennial, the substance of which, in certain respects, has not been included in the several publications on the Centennial, and this is set forth in his preface to the report.

Dr. Tatum has graciously given his permission to reproduce the preface.

As the first century of American independence approached its close, a number of individuals and organizations suggested ways whereby the centennial year of 1876 might most appropriately be celebrated. Of these proposals, that of the representatives of the Franklin Institute of Philadelphia for an International Exhibition in their city received the most favorable attention. Accordingly, on February 24, 1870, the City of Philadelphia, the Board of Managers of the Franklin Institute, and the Commonwealth of Pennsylvania together memorialized Congress to "stimulate a pilgrimage to the Mecca of America Nationality, the Home of American Independence," by authorizing an International Exhibition of Arts, Manufactures, and Products of the Soil and Mine which in its form would illustrate "the unparalleled advancement in science and art and all the various appliances of human ingenuity for the refinement and comfort of man" it was believed the nineteenth century afforded. In March of the following year the United States Centennial Commission was created by an act of Congress, and subsequent legislation provided for a Board of Finance composed of twenty-five directors with authority to issue capital stock to the limit of ten million dollars. By the summer of 1873 arrangements had progressed sufficiently far for President Grant to issue a proclamation declaring that the exhibition would be held in 1876 and inviting foreign nations to participate. On the following day, July 4, 1873, the Commissioners of Fairmount Park made available 450 acres of land bordering on the Schuylkill River and extending from Lansdowne to Belmont avenues.

The idea for an international exhibition was not of course either new or original. Historians would trace its origin at least as far back as the fairs of antiquity and the Middle Ages, but the proponents of the Philadelphia Centennial undoubtedly had in mind more recent examples. In the second half of the nineteenth century important international exhibitions had been held at London (1851 and 1862), New York (1853), Paris (1855 and 1867), and Vienna (1873). Together these offered valuable precedent and experience upon which the commissioners might draw as they made their plans for an exhibition in Philadelphia.

Following the pattern set by the Crystal Palace that Joseph Paxton had designed for the London Exhibition of 1851, the Committee on Plans and Architecture first thought in terms of a single building to cover twenty-five acres, a portion of which was to be so designed that it might remain as a permanent structure to be known as Memorial Hall. It was also intended that a second temporary building would be constructed nearby and that this would serve during the Exhibition as an art gallery. These, in brief, were the terms of the first unlimited competition the Committee announced in 1873. The authors of the ten best projects were each to receive $1000 and to be given the privilege of submitting designs in a second and final competition.

By July 15, 1873, when the first competition closed, 43 designs had been received; the majority were from Philadelphia and New York, but some came from as far away as San Francisco and New Orleans. Unknown amateurs were represented as well as such established architects as John McArthur, Jr., architect of the Philadelphia City Hall, and Calvert Vaux of New York, principal architect of the Museum of Natural History in that city and the designer, with Frederick Law Olmsted, of Central Park. Plans varied considerably among circles, squares and rectangles and, in recognition of the patriotic basis of the exposition, the star received rather more prominence than was perhaps architecturally desirable. Many of the designs showed the influence of the earlier European exhibitions and most of them included a large central dome or some form of a tower that would serve to give the building an appearance of dignity and importance, while at the same time affording the visitor who ascended it a view of park and city. Fortunately, all of the entries were photographed and a few of the original drawings are preserved at the Historical Society of Pennsylvania.

Of the ten architects who were selected to submit designs in the final competition, four were awarded additional premiums. The "pavilion plan" embodied in the entry of Calvert Vaux and George Radford of New York was favorably received, but its authors did not place because the judges considered that they had not complied with the specifications of the competition. Fourth place went to the brothers H. A. and J. P. Sims of Philadelphia (designers of the first Girard Avenue bridge) who received an award of $1000 for a design that included a permanent memorial building which somewhat resembled a Gothic cathedral. McArthur and Wilson, also of Philadelphia, placed third with an impressive building of brick and iron surmounted by a tower 500 feet high, which, had it been built, would have been at that time the highest structure in the world. For an ornate Neo-Baroque design still another Philadelphian, Samuel Sloan, was given second place and an additional premium of $3000. But the proposal which included the largest dome and the most elaborate decoration was submitted by the firm of Collins and Autenrieth and to them the Committee awarded first place and a prize of $4000.

Grandeur is likely to be expensive, however, and when the commissioners found that the winning design would cost at least ten million dollars to build, they decided to abandon the original plan to erect one large structure in favor of a variety of smaller buildings devoted to specific purposes. There was precedent for this decision since a number of separate pavilions had been tried with considerable success at the Paris Exposition of 1867. In the end the Exhibition was to be made up of over two hundred structures of various kinds, the design and disposition of which may most easily be studied in the handsome model still preserved in the basement of Memorial Hall.

Considerations of cost probably also played a major part in the commission's decision to dispense with the services of the architects who had placed in the competition and to rely instead on those already in the employ of the commission or who were practicing in nearby cities. James H. Windrim, who had probably been too busy designing the Masonic Temple in Philadelphia to enter the first competition, was engaged to supply the plans for Agricultural Hall. This was a large

"Gothic" structure built of wood and glass on the north side of the grounds not far from Belmont Mansion. Although Windrim's building covered 10 1/4 acres and provided 236,572 feet of exhibition space, it ranked third in size among the major structures planned for the Exhibition.

It was estimated, in fact, that half the population of Philadelphia could have been accommodated at one time in the Main Exhibition Building (Industrial Hall), which formed a large rectangle 1876 feet long in front of Memorial Hall. Both this building and the similar, but smaller Machinery Hall, located to the west, were designed by Henry Pettit and Joseph M. Wilson. Unlike many of the other structures of the Centennial, the Main Exhibition Building and Machinery Hall were largely devoid of decorative details and their essentially utilitarian character may have been suggested to Pettit by his study of earlier European exhibitions as well as by the engineer's training which he and Wilson shared. The latter had gained his experience in the employ of Pennsylvania Railroad and after the Centennial—and perhaps largely as a result of his work there—founded the firm of Wilson Brothers, which during the next quarter of a century designed many important structures including, most notably, the original portion of the Broad Street Station in Philadelphia.

Like Agricultural Hall, Industrial Hall and Machinery Hall were temporary structures and both were demolished shortly after the close of the Exhibition. Horticultural Hall and Memorial Hall, on the other hand, were intended from the first as permanent buildings which would remain as ornaments to the Park and monuments of the exhibition and it is therefore surprising that their design was turned over to a young and largely unknown engineer in the employ of the Fairmount Park Commission. This was Hermann Joseph Schwarzmann, who was born in Munich, Germany, in 1846, and who had come to Philadelphia in 1868. In addition to the two large permanent structures, Schwarzmann also designed (or helped to design) at least a dozen smaller buildings, including the Women's Pavilion, Judges Hall, the Carriage Building, and the Pennsylvania State Building. After the close of the Exhibition, Schwarzmann moved to New York and there in partnership with Albert Buchman continued to practice architecture until shortly before his death in 1891.

Until its demolition in 1955, Horticultural Hall remained one of the most interesting and important examples of nineteenth-century architecture. In its use of glass and iron it recalled the building Paxton had designed for the London Exhibition twenty-five years before and thereby typified the interest of the period in new materials and methods of construction. The Moorish style used for decorative details was also a reminder of the romantic love of the exotic that had colored American taste throughout the preceding half century. In this and other respects Schwarzmann's building looked to the past, rather than to the future; it was perhaps the last great building of its kind that would be devoted to the subject of horticulture, for the second century of

PLATE 27.   Memorial Hall in the Centennial Exhibition. H. J. Schwarzmann, architect.

America's independence would see her transformed from a nation concerned predominantly with agriculture to one engaged largely in industry. Even in 1876 Machinery Hall with its great Corliss engine was challenging Horticultural Hall and the various agricultural exhibits for the interest of the visitors to the Centennial.

By far the most substantial and elaborate structure on the Exhibition grounds—and the only one of importance which remains standing today—was the building known then, as now, as Memorial Hall (Plate 27). Standing north of the Main Exhibition Hall in the eastern portion of the Centennial enclosure, it is situated on a commanding rise of ground 112 feet above the nearby Schuylkill River. The million and a half dollars which the building cost was provided by the Commonwealth of Pennsylvania and the City of Philadelphia, since it was intended from the first that it would remain either as the home of the Pennsylvania Museum of Art or possibly as a legislative hall, should it later be determined to move the capital of the Commonwealth from Harrisburg to Philadelphia, as some had proposed.

For his principal material Schwarzmann chose granite and combined with it brick, iron, and glass to create what was then considered a permanent and fireproof building. To emphasize further its importance, Memorial Hall was set off from the rest of the buildings of the Centennial by being placed upon a broad terrace approximately six feet above the surrounding area and bordered by a stone balustrade, since removed. At either end of the steps leading to the terrace were placed the two large bronze groups representing Pegasus led by the Muses (Plate 28) that had been brought from Vienna some years before and

PLATE 28.   Memorial Hall, showing sculpture at the main entrance.

presented to the Fairmount Park Commission by R. H. Gratz. Thirteen more steps, which presumably commemorate in their number the original American colonies, lead from the terrace to the main (and originally the only) entrance on the south. Access to the building is through three large (15' by 40') arched doorways closed by iron doors to which are affixed bronze panels decorated with the arms of the states and territories. The granite piers at either side of the entrance are crowned by massive zinc figures representing Science and Art, the work of A. M. J. Müller, a German artist then residing in Philadelphia. The same sculptor also modeled in clay the zinc figures that represent the four quarters of the globe and are appropriately seated at each of the corners of the square dome of iron and glass which rises 150 feet above the floor of the center hall (Plate 29). The large zinc figure crowning the dome was intended by Müller to represent Columbia.

On either side of the main entrance are arcades that connect with corner pavilions, each 36 feet square and lighted by two large (12 1/2' by 30') windows. Originally these arcades were open and through them could be seen the flowers and fountains of a small court, but in more recent years the arcades have been closed and the courts roofed over. The north façade, which during the Centennial faced the Art Annex, resembles the south front except that the place of the open arcades is taken by windows that light a series of 13 small rooms intended for the display of works of art or to serve as small studios. On the east and west the wall that joins the corner pavilions is pierced on the exterior with niches for sculpture. Eagles with spread wings, the symbol of America, once rested on each of the corners of the four pavilions above the frieze of sculptured stars.

On entering from the south, the visitor to Memorial Hall finds himself in a spacious vestibule from which wide doorways lead into a central hall 83 feet square (Plate 30). Here were received the distinguished visitors who came to view what soon came to be called simply "The Great Exhibition." On the east and west of the central hall were rooms nearly 100 feet long, so that when the doors were opened, there could be formed a grand gallery capable of holding 8000 persons, in 1876 a considerably larger number than could be accommodated anywhere else in America. This is not to imply, of course, that during the Centennial these rooms were thus combined; then on the west side wooden partitions separated the paintings sent by Great Britain from those exhibited by the United States, while in the east gallery similar temporary barriers divided the work of French artists from those of Germany. In this way available wall space was increased to nearly 88,000 square feet. Sculpture was confined largely to the open courts and the four corner pavilions.

Throughout Memorial Hall many of the walls were covered with bas-reliefs, and many of the floors, which cover an area of approximately 1 1/2 acres, were inlaid with marble tiles. This was grandeur and size to which in 1876 very few Americans were accustomed. To admire its reputed beauties and to be amazed by the assortment of art objects

PLATE 29.   Interior of dome in the Great Hall, Memorial Hall.

PLATE 30.   Great Hall, Memorial Hall.

that filled Memorial Hall and overflowed into the Art Annex behind, probably as many as ten million persons visited the Exhibition between the opening on May 10 and the date of closing, November 10. There was no doubt that the Philadelphia Centennial was at least a popular success!

Contemporary accounts describe Memorial Hall as being in "the Modern Renaissance style," and later architectural historians would probably interpret this to mean the art of France as then taught by the influential Ecole des Beaux-Arts and seen here through the eyes of the young German immigrant, Hermann Schwarzmann. Perhaps some elements of the design were suggested by the competition drawings referred to above, and the influence of earlier European exhibitions may also be assumed. But whatever his sources, Schwarzmann managed to create a design which, although perhaps somewhat heavy in its total effect, has considerable architectural distinction.

In his *Guide to the Centennial* Thompson Westcott expressed his regret that in a few months all the buildings which had sprung up "as if by magic" would in the same fashion disappear, leaving only Horticultural Hall and Memorial Hall "to tell the story of the greatness of the Exhibition to succeeding generations." Probably more was destined to remain of the Centennial than Westcott realized; the Catholic Total Abstinence Fountain is still in place, as is the house erected by Ohio nearby (Plate 31). Both the Wisconsin Building, which

PLATE 31. Ohio House in the Centennial Exhibition. Heard Brothers, architects, Cleveland. Stones of the building are inscribed with names of quarries and towns in Ohio.

was moved to Bala Cynwyd, and the half-timbered British buildings survived until well into the twentieth century. Those may be mistaken who believe they have traced peregrinations of the Japanese Pavilion to final service as the Strafford railroad station, but there is no doubt that the Maryland Building was relocated in Druid Hill Park, Baltimore, or that others were made to serve a variety of functions at sites as far away as New Haven, New York, Atlantic City, and Cape May. But Westcott was undoubtedly right that for most people Memorial Hall would remain, as those who built and named it intended from the first that it should, the principal symbol of the Exhibition which celebrated the first century of American independence.

The report of Hatfield, Martin, and White was entitled "The adaptation of Memorial Hall," and the building, as restored over a period of several years at a cost in excess of two million dollars, now includes an Olympic-size swimming and diving pool, a college-size basketball court, the administrative offices of the Fairmount Park Commission, quarters for the Park Guard, and the restoration of the Great Hall for city and park "events of state."

5

Some Houses in the Park

The doors that knew no shrill alarming bell,
No cursed knocker ply'd by villians hand,
Self-opened into halls, where who can tell
What elegance and grandeur wide expand,
The pride of Turkey and of Persia land?
                                    Thomson

Dr. Fiske Kimball, director of the Philadelphia Museum of Art, wrote in an introduction to the book *"The Colonial Mansions in Fairmount Park"*:*

By the middle of the [eighteenth] century the prosperous merchants of the town [Philadelphia] were no longer satisfied without a country seat, cultivated perhaps, but not for real subsistence. Recurring epidemics of yellow fever in the city made these places a cherished retreat. Thus, whether enlarged or newly built, arose the mansions of the Schuylkill. Along this lovely river each promontory of either bank soon had its house. Of these built before the Revolution the greatest

*The Colonial Mansions in Fairmount Park by Theo. B. White was published in 1933. A folio volume, it contained seven lithographic illustrations printed from stones. One hundred and twenty volumes were printed. The accounts of houses contained herein and the reproductions of five of the lithographs are from that publication. Lithographs by the author.

were Lansdowne — long destroyed — Mount Pleasant, Belmont and Woodford. Each had its special point of attraction: Belmont its magnificent plasterwork, Woodford its fine drawing-room with richly carved over-mantel, Lansdowne its double portico, Mount Pleasant its perfect symmetry with balanced out-buildings, as well as its superb Great Chamber.

The Revolution filled these places with historic memories: of Washington, Lafayette, and Rochambeau, Judge Peters's guests at Belmont, of Arnold, Peggy Shippen, and Steuben at Mount Pleasant, of Robert Morris at The Hills.

After the Revolution came the houses of a new generation: of John Penn at Solitude, Henry Pratt at Lemon Hill, Edward Shippen Burd at Ormiston, Samuel Breck at Sweetbrier, William Lewis at Strawberry, and many others. A new spirit informed their design. The influence of the Adam style in England was first felt at Solitude, with its delicate ornament. New conceptions of space appeared in the oval salon and curved staircase of Lemon Hill. The years around eighteen hundred were a second heyday for the great houses of the Schuylkill.

WOODFORD

In a period that demanded charm, wit, and beauty of its ladies, Rebecca Franks moved as a prominent personality in that group of beautiful women whose society has become legendary in Philadelphia. It was the time of the occupation of the city by the British forces. While Washington's army struggled with the difficulties of a bitter existence on the hills outside, the British officers settled down in security at Philadelphia to amuse themselves with a society created for a brief season by the Tory families. It was the period of the Peggy Shippen and Benedict Arnold romance. It was the year of the "Mischianza," when all the Tory ladies trooped to that colorful pageant at Joseph Wharton's place, Walnut Grove, to dance the night and morning away. In the minds of those ladies, to be a graceful hostess was instinctive and as important as the necessity of appearing in gowns of the latest mode. So sedulously were the social amenities cultivated by their coterie that it is not surprising to find Rebecca Franks writing to her sister, Mrs. Hamilton, from New York:

Bye the bye, few ladies here know how to entertain company in their own houses, unless they introduce the card table. . . . I will do our ladies — that is, the Philadelphians — the justice to say that they have more cleverness in the turn of an eye, than those of New York have in their whole composition. With what ease have I seen a Chew, an

PLATE 32.   Woodford

Oswald, and Allen, and a thousand others, entertain in a large circle of both sexes, and the conversation without the aid of cards not flag or seem the least strained or stupid.

And the charm that Rebecca and her friends of the same political persuasions expended on the British officers was consistent, if not commendable. When a young lieutenant from Maryland called on Miss Franks, and in jest wore a scarlet coat and demanded that he be accorded her favor since he wore her colors, she contemptuously replied, "How the ass glories in the lion's skin." A brilliant woman, she was as beautiful as she was intellectual. Being a letter-writer of some ability, she has left a most illuminating group of letters that form a keen commentary on the period and the people. From the lowest-ranking officer to General Howe, they all succumbed to her charm; and, in fact, the latter officer was wont to stop his horse at her house, when free of the duties of war, and spend a while to enjoy her humor. It was not until the next century, and in England, that, prematurely old and sick, she greeted General Winfield Scott with outstretched hands and the words, "Would to God, I too, had been a patriot."

She had doubtless been strengthened in her Tory convictions by the action of the government against her father, David Franks. He was a wealthy and prominent Jew, a member of the Provincial Assembly, Registrar of Wills, and subscriber to the Dancing Assembly. He had married a daughter of Peter Evans, but never deserted his hereditary faith, as has been testified by Judge Peters. A descendant of the English Jew Aaron Franks, who loaned King George of Hanover some of the costliest jewels used in the crown at that monarch's coronation, he came justly by his Tory politics. Because of these he had been appointed agent of the Crown in Philadelphia, and later became commissary of the British prisoners in American lines. He was found transmitting a letter contrary to the American cause, and was arrested and jailed by order of Benedict Arnold.

Franks had obtained Woodford from Alexander Barclay, a grandson of the famous Quaker Robert Barclay, who in turn had purchased it from the trustees of the estate of William Coleman, Judge of the Supreme Court of Pennsylvania. The land had originally been a grant from William Penn to Mary Rotchford, who deeded it to Thomas Shute. At his death it was sold, but later bought back by his son, Joseph Shute. At a sheriff's sale about 1756, Judge Coleman secured twelve acres of the property together with the small, dignified one-story house built by Thomas Shute. It is apparent from the heavy band-course or cornice just above the first-floor windows that the second floor was a later addition, and evidence indicates that it was built by Judge Coleman. It was he who added some of the fine wainscoting to the first floor. As the house now stands, modest and simple, with that lack of ornateness characteristic of the latter part of the century, it is obviously the home of a man of cultivated taste.

As a scholar, Judge Coleman became a close friend of Franklin's and a member of the famous "Junto" group, which that distinguished Philadelphian described as "the best school of philosophy, morality and politics that then existed in the province." Once a week this group of men, to which a member was admitted only on proof of the quality of his intellect, gathered to discuss morals, philosophy, politics, and art. Franklin has characterized his friend in his usual succinct language:

> And William Coleman. . .about my own age, who had the coolest, clearest head, the best heart, and the exactest morals of almost any man I ever met with. He became afterwards a merchant of great note, and one of our provincial judges. Our friendship continued without interruption to his death, upwards of forty years.

From Judge Coleman's house one can look across the river and catch a glimpse of Belmont, the house of another judge. Had the two men been contemporaneous, there doubtless would have been a close friendship due to their common interest in conversation and their congeniality of tastes.

BELMONT

There is probably no other colonial house in Philadelphia that can boast such delightful dinners, so colorful a pageant of revolutionary social life, and so quiet a charm of intimate companionship, as Belmont in Judge Peters's day. The gracious and generous hospitality of the man has become legendary. And as a setting for this, the lovely mansion in its eighteenth-century aspect reflects the character of both its owner and his guests.

When Judge Peters's father came to America in 1739, probably at the insistence of his brother, the Reverend Dr. Richard Peters, he married Mary Breitnall and soon acquired the two hundred and twenty acres forming the Belmont estate. From a grant by William Penn in 1684, the property had passed through the ownership of four individuals, and although the identity of the person who built the original part of the house group is not established as fact, it is reasonable to believe that it was accomplished before William Peters's time. He, however, immediately set about adding to the small stone house with the bay, probably in anticipation of the approaching

PLATE 33.   Belmont

birth of Richard in June 1744. Then in 1755, the large mansion facing the river was built as an addition. An old water color of 1820–1830 shows the house as it then existed, and before Joseph S. Lovering, in 1853, ruined the simple and elegant proportions by the addition of a third story. It was, before, two stories in height with a classic cornice and a hip roof. A slight projection embracing three windows was surmounted by a pediment. Eventually, a fine stairhall was added to the western side, with a simple classic doorway leading to the garden. If we refer to the diary of Hannah Callender, dated one fine day in June 1762, we get an excellent picture of the house and its spacious gardens.

> All went down to Schuylkill. Then went to William Peters's house, having some acquaintance with his wife. . .received us kindly in one wing of the house. After a while passed through a covered passage to the large hall, well furnished, the top adorned with instruments of music, coats of arms, crests, and other ornaments in stucco, its sides by paintings and statues in bronze. From the front of this hall, you have a prospect bordered by the Jerseys like a blue ridge. A broad walk of English cherry trees leads down to the river. The doors of the house opening opposite admit a prospect of the path over a broad gravel walk to a large handsome summer house on a green. From the windows a vista is terminated by an obelisk. On the right you enter a labyrinth of hedge of low cedar and spruce. In the middle stands a statue of Apollo. In the garden are statues of Fame, Mercury, Diana with urns. In the midst is a Chinese temple for a summer house.

Most of this Richard Peters saw in the making, slowly and by stages, as houses then were created. All of his early life he had been in contact with influential men whom his father had had at Belmont as his guests, so that, after his studies at the College of Philadelphia and his admittance to the bar, his rise to prominence was rapid. He was made a captain during the war, but was relieved of this post by Congress to become Secretary of the Board of War. As a member of the Assembly, he gained the speaker's chair in the House, and finally succeeded his neighbor, Judge Lewis of Strawberry Mansion, as judge on the bench of the United States District Court. He was an accomplished linguist, an undoubted intellectual with a wide reputation for wit, and through his extensive acquaintance in the army and at the bar, he attracted to Belmont many of the notable figures that came to Philadelphia in the early days of the Federal government. His neighbor, Samuel Breck of Sweetbrier, has written at length of his personality.

The playfulness of his conversation always enlivened by flashes of the gayest pleasantry was forever quick and unrestrained and varied by casts of true humour, sometimes as broad and well enacted as the most exaggerated farce, and at others convolved in double meaning, fit only for the ready perception of the most practiced ear and polished taste. . . .Unceremonious, communicative, friendly.

And aside from the elegant entertainment of distinguished guests, of which he was doubtless a master, he could be the easy, interesting friend of the same great figures who graced his table on the more ceremonious occasions. Just such a friend, for example, he was to Washington, and of this relationship Mr. Breck has also written.

When a morning of leisure permitted that great man [Washington] to drive to Belmont. . .it was his constant habit to do so. There, sequestered from the world, the torments and cares of his business, Washington would enjoy. . .a wholly unceremonious intercourse with the judge, walking for hours side by side, in the beautiful gardens of Belmont, beneath the dark shade of lofty hemlocks placed there by his ancestors a century ago. In these romantic grounds stood a chestnut tree reared from a Spanish nut planted by the hand of Washington. . . it was cherished at Belmont as a precious evidence of the intimacy that existed between those distinguished men.

That austere critic, John Quincy Adams, whose praise of men and events was used sparingly, and only when deserved, is almost enthusiastic in his account of a dinner at Belmont in company with Lafayette, Samuel Breck, and others.

Miss Peters, the judge's daughter, who keeps his house, was the only lady present. It was a cheering time. Judge Peters is upwards of four-score years of age, in sound, healthy, good spirits, and of conversation sparkling with wit and humour.

We are, indeed, indebted to the first two Adamses for their comments on the owners of two great mansions on the Schuylkill. As different as the New England father was from his son, just so differ their searching comments on the occasions of a visit by the son to Belmont, and by the father to that grand old house across the river, Mount Pleasant.

MOUNT PLEASANT

John Adams visited John Macpherson at Mount Pleasant in 1775, and his remarks of admiration and sympathy are from one who had a modicum of

PLATE 34.   Mount Pleasant

the rebel in him, concerning another who had a decidedly aggressive and rebellious character.

He [Macpherson] has the most elegant seat in Pennsylvania, a clever Scotch wife and two pretty daughters. His seat is on the banks of the Schuylkill. He has been nine times wounded in battle, is an old sea-commander, made a fortune by privateering, had an arm twice shot off, shot through the leg.

The interlude in John Macpherson's life beginning at the time he left his clan of Clunie in Scotland and up to the period in which he built Mount Pleasant reads much like an imaginative adventure tale for boys. Apparently his presence in Philadelphia was not attended with any note until 1757, when he assumed command of a privateer, the *Britannia,* equipped with twenty guns. The war with France was quite active at that time, and the pirating of French commerce was attractive to sailormen both as adventure and as a means of acquiring a fortune. The Scottish captain was disappointed in the latter feature of the *Britannia's* first voyage under his command. They met a Frenchman of thirty-six guns, and in the ensuing conflict the *Britannia's* decks literally ran blood; Macpherson lost his right arm, and his two junior officers were disabled, with seventy of the crew wounded or killed. In the very next year, however, he took the battered *Britannia* back to sea, and the one-armed captain made his fortune. In the next two years he took at least twenty-seven prizes, which netted him a substantial profit. The excitement and danger attendant on the acquisition of his money doubtless increased the legendary desire of all sailormen and soldiers for a quiet and permanent retreat. Thus, when a peace had been made between France, Spain, and England, he returned to Philadelphia and sought a place for his home.

The east bank of the Schuylkill was then practically a natural and untouched forest. High on a hill where he might see a great expanse of river, he purchased about sixty acres and built a fine mansion. He had doubtless at some time sailed the *Britannia* into Chesapeake Bay, and perhaps a short way up the James and Potomac. There he may have seen Mount Airy, Carter's Grove, Mount Vernon, and other Virginia houses, for his estate is planned rather in the manner of those Southern houses. The mansion forms the focus of a group of stables and offices that bear a definite plan relation to the main house, the latter group of buildings, together with a hedge of English box, forming an imposing forecourt. In the same manner as at Carter's Grove on the James, three terraces have been carved out of the hill descending to the river on the west. Across the formal garden is a Chinese temple used as a summer house, perhaps inspired by the one at Belmont across the river. To his place he gave the name of Clunie, from his clan in Scotland, but later changed it to Mount Pleasant.

Unfortunately, Captain Macpherson apparently spent his money in much the same impulsive manner in which he gained it, for by 1770 he had to rent the house to Alvaro Deornelles at seventy pounds a month, an extraordinarily high price when houses in Philadelphia were considered dear at a hundred per annum. Later it was leased to Don Juan de Mirailles, the Spanish envoy. In 1779 the house was sold, subject to the lease and a heavy mortgage, to Major General Benedict Arnold, who purchased it as a wedding

PLATE 35.   Mount Pleasant interior

PLATE 36.   Mount Pleasant interior

gift for his lovely bride, Peggy Shippen. From this fact the house has often been misnamed the "Benedict Arnold Mansion." It is doubtful whether Arnold and his bride ever occupied it, and, in fact, the gift was little more than a gesture, for according to Judge Peters of Belmont, the money that Arnold used to buy the equity was converted from army funds.

The house seemed to have a strange destiny that dictated continuous association with fighting men. Arnold's estate was sold by the state to Colonel Richard Hampton, and in 1792 the house was sold again to a revolutionary officer, later appointed judge in the Common Pleas Court, General Jonathan Williams, whose family retained it until 1853. Between Colonel Hampton's ownership and that of General Williams, the Baron von Steuben leased it. Mr. Breck tells an amusing story of this latter occupant of Mount Pleasant. It seems that Lafayette had been given a doctor's degree by some New England college, and the doughty German general had snorted in disgust. One day he halted a troop of his dragoons outside that same college town, and instructed them thus: "You shall spur de horse vel and ride troo the town like de debbil, for if dey catch you dey make one doctor of you."

John Adams erred little, if at all, in describing Mount Pleasant as the "most elegant seat in Pennsylvania." There is a simple spaciousness of plan and proportion that forms an excellent setting for the delicately carved woodwork. This has been utilized in those places where it best accentuates the simplicity of the wood moldings and cornices. It was built at a time when the rocaille or "French taste" was fashionable and general. It was, too, a time when the city was the metropolis of America, and when Philadelphia craftsmanship had reached a peak of brilliance.

The story of the house with its successive occupants seems strangely synonymous with the history of the period. Built, as it was, in the period of unrest that preceded and continued through the war with England, it is perhaps proper that some of its occupants should have been leading figures of the period. Unlike Belmont, it has not descended from one generation to another of the same family, so that it has missed the care and affection that is thus brought to an old house; rather, it had been created by an adventurer, and not until two decades after the war did it gain a constant companion. Its loveliness and feeling seem fitted to be a background for a graceful figure and gracious mind, as Belmont was for Judge Peters, Westover for William Byrd, and Sweetbrier, with its unostentatious charm, for Samuel Breck.

SWEETBRIER

Almost directly across the river from Mount Pleasant, Samuel Breck chose

PLATE 37. Sweetbrier

the site for his house. In his description of the site and the prospect there is
the quiet delight of a man who has chosen and built well, and further, feels
that he has created a house as a complement to himself, than which there is
scarcely a finer achievement in architecture.

> The mansion. . .I built in 1797. . . .The prospect consists of the river,
> animated by its great trade carried on in boats of about thirty tons,
> drawn by horses; of a beautiful sloping lawn, terminating at the river,
> now nearly four hundred yards wide opposite the portico; of
> side-screened woods; of gardens, greenhouses, etc. Sweetbrier is the
> name of my villa.

To understand further the gentleman who lived in Sweetbrier, and to
savor with him in imagination some of the exquisite contentment he enjoyed
there, another quotation from his journal will disclose a mind appreciative of
the simple philosophies of life. After mentioning that he had in January
1808 — the thirty-seventh year of his life — been visiting a lady of "many
excellent qualities" who had been complaining of her ill-fortune at being
deprived of a part of a substantial income, he continues: "For my own share,
I confess I draw from this comparison a fund of contentment which my
situation abstractedly would not seem susceptible of; and in fact, what is my
position?" This self-put question he answers frankly and simply, and thereby
reveals to us an admirable character.

> Reared by the most indulgent of parents, surrounded by every luxury
> and comfort which America could afford, moving in a vortex of gay and
> fashionable company, I found myself at twenty-six years of age seques-
> tered from them all and confined to a sober, solitary country life; my
> fortune once competent and easy, reduced to a standard of a decent
> subsistence; bereft of the means of receiving my friends, and childless
> until now; placed alone with Mrs. Breck to exercise our philosophy and
> learn to laugh. . . .Thus I have spent the last ten years, and I can in
> truth declare. . .they have been filled with that measure of happiness
> which it is proper for us to taste.

Born in Boston, Mr. Breck had gone abroad for part of his education, and
there met some of the central figures of France's revolution. Returning to
this country, he settled in Philadelphia for reasons necessitated by his
business. At the age of twenty-six he built Sweetbrier, and entered into an
intimacy with his neighbor, Judge Peters of Belmont, and many of the
prominent people who made Philadelphia's society the most brilliant in the
country during the early days of the Federal government. Of these people,
and of many of the French refugees who sought peace and security here, he

has left charming descriptions and anecdotes among his journals and notes. That he was possessed of a charming wit, was an agreeable dinner companion, and was attractive to the intellects of his time is amply testified by the houses he attended and by his own guests.

He had that leisurely turn of mind and conservative tastes which fit so nicely with the spirit of his house, and are in fact so necessary to the creation of an eighteenth-century mansion. It is partly this spirit that appears in these slightly indignant lines — to quote again from his journal — that attracts us and leads us to wonder at the savoir faire so evident in the society of that century.

> Undoubtedly a traveler will be able to go from Baltimore to New York by the light of a summer's sun when the locomotives shall be placed on the Amboy railroad. . . . The rich and the poor, the educated and the ignorant, the polite and the vulgar, all herd together in this modern improvement in traveling. Master and servant sleep head and points. . . sit in each others' laps. . .and all this for the sake of doing very uncomfortably in two days what might be done delightfully in eight or ten. Talk of ladies. . .on a railroad car! There are none. I never felt like a gentleman there, and I cannot perceive a semblance of gentility in anyone who makes part of the traveling mob. . . .To restore herself to caste, let a lady move in select company at five miles an hour and take her meals in comfort at a good inn, where she may dine decently. . . . After all the old-fashioned way of five or six miles an hour with one's own horses and carriage, with liberty to dine decently...and be master of one's movements, with the delight of seeing the country and getting along rationally, is the mode to which I cling, and which will be adapted again by the generations of after times.

Sweetbrier is not one of the large mansions, nor does it possess any of the polite ostentation of Mount Pleasant. Built toward the end of the century, it illustrates the period of Colonial architecture, which was, perhaps, the most charming. By that time decoration had achieved a delightful delicacy of feeling that bespeaks a sophistication never expressed before the last decade of the century. Life was easy and simple, and although the Federal government was experiencing its first growing pains, society moved gracefully and interestingly in the capital of the new republic; and certainly the mansions of this late period, with their feeling of spaciousness and quiet dignity, admirably set off their owners.

Indeed, it would be difficult to find elsewhere a more interesting or elegant group of houses than those clustered together on the hills forming the small and somewhat intimate Schuylkill valley. And our interest in the houses is enhanced and heightened by the character of the small and intimate group who owned them. They were all prominent figures at the bar, in business, or in the army, and all had keen interests outside their general pursuits. Not unlike the majority of interesting people, they had slight personal eccentricities, and these, together with their wit, must surely have made the dinners of the time altogether delightful affairs. Perhaps the greatest eccentric and keenest wit among them, excepting only Judge Peters, was Judge William Lewis, who built Strawberry Mansion, up and across the river from Sweetbrier.

STRAWBERRY

One has only to glance at the portrait of William Lewis to realize that he was an extremely ugly man, but with that ugliness that attracts and in an agreeable person becomes a mark of distinction. On closer study the eyes have a sparkle that is confirmed in the mouth, which always seems ready to smile in appreciation of a good story. According to a contemporary, he was "destitute of almost all dimensions but length" and was "immensely proud of the altitude and length of his nose." The latter fact is perhaps attested by the prominence Stuart has accorded it in his portrait. Apparently he was an excellent lawyer and capable of vehement argument in court. A colleague wrote "that he would sometimes rise to the fervor and energy of a sibyl."

However, when not engaged in legal affairs he was apt to be found "quizzing or joking or mooting or smoking, generally in a state of unrest." And his "seegar" was one of his eccentricities upon which his friends smiled indulgently. An inveterate smoker, his habit was allowed in company where in anyone else it would have been a distressing exhibition of bad manners. In fact, a friend was sufficiently amazed by his constant smoking to observe that it seemed not "like an accommodation to health or taste but like submission to conquest by an external power."

He was born a Quaker, in Chester County, and educated in the Society. This, however, did not prevent his entertaining strong opinions and acting entirely in accordance with them. Philadelphia at the time was affording a security for those upper-class people who had had to leave France in consequence of the Revolution. Feeling in the city was keen and on the whole sympathetic. Judge Lewis had little taste for the Revolutionists, and when they finally dispensed with powder and queues and took to pantaloons, he indignantly expressed his disfavor by wearing knee breeches with powdered hair and a queue all his life.

In the early years of his gradual progress from a law office through the legislature, the Convention for the Constitution, the office of the United States District Attorney, to President Judge of the District Court, he carried

PLATE 38. Strawberry

the same high feelings in his defense of pacifist Quakers. These good people were often unjustly accused as Tories or traitors. Some of these cases he undertook to defend without remuneration, receiving instead an enhanced reputation. From this he turned his attention to the slavery controversy. As a vigorous opponent of slavery he finally secured the passage of a bill in the legislature abolishing slavery in Pennsylvania. He is generally credited with forcing the enactment of the first laws of this kind in the world. In appreciation of this latter act, the Society of Friends presented him with a service of silver.

The mansion, constructed in the same period as Sweetbrier, is in much the same character. The original part of the house — the center portion — is, indeed, very much like Mr. Breck's house. On the interior, the plan being similar to those of Sweetbrier and Mount Pleasant, there is the characteristic simplicity of treatment, with the ornament delicately conceived and executed. It remained for the next owner, also a judge, Joseph Hemphill, to add two wings to either end of the small and unpretentious house in 1827 and 1829. This made Summerton, as it was then called, one of the larger houses on the Schuylkill.

Judge Hemphill was a cultivated man, mild of manner, a vestryman in three churches, and interested in divers institutions such as the Philosophical Society, the Academy of the Fine Arts, and the Dancing Assembly. From the manufacture of fine porcelain, he turned to the cultivation of the gardens already begun by Judge Lewis. It is from this love of gardening, which included small fruits, that the mansion eventually became known as Strawberry, for he established the exceedingly fine strawberry beds in the gardens. Under the combined efforts of the judge and his son Coleman, the house quickly achieved a reputation for its hospitality. In fact, it has been a tradition in the family that the south wing was built to "entertain the City Troop." In common with his neighbors on the river, he possessed many friends of considerable note. Calhoun of Carolina, John Randolph of Roanoke, Carroll of Maryland, with Webster and Lafayette, were frequent visitors.

Judge Hemphill died in 1842, and the mansion was bought by a Mrs. Grimes, who ran a sort of restaurant in the old house, specializing in the fine strawberries planted by the judge. It was from these, dispensed by Mrs. Grimes, that the house became popularly known as Strawberry Mansion. Thus the old name of Summerton passed with one of the last of the men who gave that part of the Schuylkill a tradition it can never lose.

They were men of a different vision, those men who built the mansions of Fairmount Park. The glory of the eighteenth century was theirs. It was a time when this country achieved a fineness in art. Graceful manners and a gracious philosophy combined with wit and a leisurely love of living produced intellects that demanded character in a house. A delicate sense of proportion toward life was expressed in their creations. Their houses reflect and are reflectors. More than this can scarcely be sought for in art.

6

The Fairmount Park Art Association

Dr. Leslie W. Miller, D.F.A., LL.D., onetime secretary of the Fairmount Park Art Association, said in a paper read before the association:

> The true measure of a community is the measure of the things for which it cares and that the record of such greatness of spirit and such nobleness of purpose as it possesses are embodied in the work it leaves behind: that the memory and influence of such worthiness as it ever develops, if it lives at all, is perpetuated by its art alone. So that no better service can be rendered to the community in which we happen to live, than the promotion in every possible way of those forms of culture and the cherishing of those ideals, which find expression in art.

The Fairmount Park Art Association is in truth a unique organization. It brought the work of many famous sculptors to adorn the park; it commissioned the architects of the parkway entrance to the park (Plate 39); it encouraged the design of the Independence Hall Mall; and it used its influence in many ways for the betterment of Philadelphia. I venture to say that there is no similar organization in this country.

Extraordinary as is the Art Association, equally so was its founding. It came into being in 1871, just four years after the park was commissioned by

PLATE 39. Benjamin Franklin Parkway from City Hall. The Museum is at the end of the parkway.

the Assembly. Two men in their early twenties and good friends conceived the Art Association; they were Charles H. Howell and Henry K. Fox.

Charles Howell (1848-1902) from early manhood was prominently interested in state military organizations. Indeed, he died a lieutenant colonel. He was an active member of the First City Troop and an honorary member at his death. He was an active friend of, and a generous contributor to, many charities. He served on the board of trustees of the Association from its inception, as secretary from 1886 to 1900, and as president for the last two years of his life.

Henry Fox (1847-1930) attended Philadelphia public schools and took his degree in law at the University of Pennsylvania. He was the son of Daniel M. Fox, Mayor of Philadelphia, 1869-1871. He was a trustee of the association from the beginning and served as treasurer and later as vice-president.

In the founding of the association, fifteen gentlemen consented to act as temporary officers and trustees. A constitution and by-laws were prepared, the preamble to which reads in part:

> Therefore, we. . . have formed ourselves into a society. . . which society shall have for its object the accumulation of a fund, by means of annual contributions of small fixed sums of money by the members thereof, and by legacies, donations, etc., which fund shall be devoted to and employed in adorning Fairmount Park with works of art, either of a memorial nature or otherwise.

In June 1871 a subscription book was opened and soon over two hundred became members of the association. Anthony J. Drexel became president and held that position until his death in 1893. It should be noted that he founded and endowed Drexel Institute (now Drexel University).

The first major action of the association in providing sculpture for the park was the commissioning of Alexander Milne Calder for an equestrian statue of Major General George Gordon Meade, who won the battle of Gettysburg. This statue is north of Memorial Hall. The state legislature appropriated $5,000 toward the cost and the association contributed an additional $5,000. By Act of Congress the federal government donated twenty twelve-pound bronze cannon for the casting of the statue. The unveiling of the sculpture took place in 1887.

But before that the association was actively acquiring sculpture. At the first annual meeting announcement was made of the acquisition of *Two Hudson Bay Wolves* by Edward Kemeys. Then in 1875 *The Dying Lioness* by Wilhelm Wolff of Berlin was placed at the north entrance to the zoo.

PLATE 40. City Hall is at the east end of the parkway.

PLATE 41. The Philadelphia Museum of Art. Zantzinger and Borie and Horace Trumbauer, architects.

PLATE 42. The north wing of the Museum.

PLATE 43.   The Rodin Museum on the parkway. Paul P. Cret and Jacques
architects.

PLATE 44.   The Free Library on the parkway. Horace Trumbauer, architect.

PLATE 45. A Park guardhouse. This is now on the parkway but was originally on the East River Drive.

ONE COUNTRY
ONE CONSTITUTION
ONE DESTINY

EACH FOR HIMSELF GATHERED UP
THE CHERISHED PURPOSES OF LIFE
ITS AIMS AND AMBITIONS
ITS DEAREST AFFECTIONS
AND FLUNG ALL WITH LIFE ITSELF
INTO THE SCALE OF BATTLE

PLATE 46. Civil War Soldiers and Sailors Memorial on the parkway. Hermon Atkins
MacNeil, sculptor. Lord and Hewlett, architects.

ALL THE
WORLD'S A STAGE
AND ALL THE
MEN AND WOMEN
MERELY PLAYERS

SHAKESPEARE MEMORIAL

PLATE 47. Shakespeare Memorial on the parkway. Alexander Stirling Calder, sculptor.
Eyre and McIlvain, architects.

PLATE 48.   Logan Circle Fountain on the parkway. Alexander Stirling Calder, sculptor.

PLATE 49. Fountain of the Sea Horses. Gift of the Italian government, 1928. Christopher Untenberger, sculptor.

PLATE 50.   Catholic Total Abstinence Fountain. Herman Kirn, sculptor.

PLATE 51.   Washington Monument on the parkway. Rudolf Siemering, sculptor. Horace Trumbauer, architect.

It has been said here that the association brought to Fairmount Park the works of many famous sculptors. Let us note a few of them, for space will not allow mention of all of them. (Detailed mention with photographs of the sculptors and their work can be seen in the volume *Fairmount Art Association, Fiftieth Anniversary, 1921*, available at the Library Company of Philadelphia, from which much of this history of the association has been obtained.)

John J. Boyle modeled in bronze the *Stone Age in America*, showing an Indian mother defending her children from an attack by bears. It is in the west park. *A Lioness Carrying to Her Young a Wild Boar* by Auguste Cain is near the Lincoln Monument. Emmanuel Frémiet is represented by the equestrian statue of *Jeanne d'Arc* (Plate 52). A heroic bust of James A. Garfield (Plate 53) by Augustus St. Gaudens, with Stanford White as architect, and *The Pilgrim* (Plate 54) by the same sculptor are great contributions to the park. There is a bronze equestrian statue of General U. S. Grant (Plate 55) the figure of which is by Daniel Chester French and the horse by Edward C. Potter. The pedestal was designed by architect Frank Miles Day. The bronze sundial near the location of the former Horticultural Hall is by Alexander Stirling Calder. Frederic Remington was the sculptor of the equestrian statue *Cowboy* (Plate 56) on the East River Drive near the Girard Avenue Bridge. There are two delightful sculptures by Albert Laessle, one, *Penguins*, in front of the Bird House in the zoo and the other, *Goat*, in Rittenhouse Square, the pedestal of which was designed by Milton Medary, architect. Also in the square is the *Goose Girl* by Paul Manship; it is in the pool of the fountain.

Richard Smith provided a legacy in his will of $500,000 for a *Monumental memorial to Pennsylvania's Military and Naval Officers and Men Distinguished for Gallantry in the late Civil War of the United States* (Plate 57). This memorial, consisting of two arches and columns and containing fourteen statues and busts, stands at the east end of the south Concourse near Memorial Hall. The sculpture is the work of twelve artists, including such distinguished men as Daniel Chester French, Alexander Stirling Calder, and Charles Grafly. The architects were James H. Windrim and his son John. One of the busts is that of James Windrim. It is a rare thing for an architect to have his modeled likeness adorning a piece of his work. The memorial was fifteen years in building, being finished in 1912.

Ellen Phillips Samuel came from a family deeply interested in Philadelphia, who were generous contributors to scientific, patriotic, and philanthropic societies. Her father was a distinguished member of the Philadelphia bar; her uncle, one of the most public-spirited men of his time, was president of the Academy of Music and of the Fairmount Park Commission.

PLATE 52. *Jeanne d'Arc.* Emmanuel Frémiet, sculptor.

PLATE 53. *James A. Garfield.* Augustus St. Gaudens, sculptor. Stanford White, architect.

PLATE 54. *The Pilgrim.* Augustus St. Gaudens, sculptor.

PLATE 55. *General U. S. Grant.* Figure by Daniel Chester French, horse by Edward C. Potter, sculptors. Pedestal by Frank Miles Day, architect.

PLATE 56. *Cowboy*. Frederic Remington, sculptor.

PLATE 57. Monumental memorial to Pennsylvania's Military and Naval Officers and Men Distinguished for Gallantry in the late Civil War of the United States.

Mrs. Samuel and her husband, J. Bunford Samuel, had for many years been intensely interested in the affairs of the association. When she died in 1913 at the age of sixty-four, she left her entire estate, upon the death of Mr. Samuel, to the association. That estate amounted to nearly $800,000. In the annual report for 1913 the association resolved . . . "that the Board of Trustees of the Fairmount Park Art Association has received with much satisfaction notice of the munificent bequest of Mrs. J. Bunford Samuel, which will provide funds for a comprehensive and dignified treatment of a noble theme — the history of America symbolized in a system of statuary in Fairmount Park — which will continue for all time the influence of the Association in promoting the aims for which it exists" (Plates 58, 59, 60).

It was a magnificent gift and perhaps unique in its purpose in this country.

A Samuel Memorial Committee was promptly appointed in 1913 and studies were made of the project, but it was impossible to proceed at that time. Upon the death of Mr. Samuel in 1929, a new committee was appointed under the chairmanship of Charles L. Borie, Jr., a distinguished architect. Paul P. Cret, architect, was selected to design the plan of the memorial. Cret's scheme consisted of three terraces on the east bank of the Schuylkill below Girard Avenue Bridge. In each of these terraces there were to be statues depicting the history of America.

Three great international sculpture exhibitions were held to select sculptors for the terraces. The first of these was in 1933 for the sculpture of the central terrace, which was not completed until 1939. The second was held in 1940 to select sculptors for the south terrace. The third took place in 1949. Credit for these exhibitions belongs to the faithful and untiring work of Henri Marceau.

The activities of this extraordinary association were not confined exclusively to furnishing sculpture for the park. Quite early in this century it turned its attention to city planning — the parkway. Henri Marceau in his address to the seventy-fifth annual meeting of the association noted that as early as 1871 a pamphlet entitled *Broad Street, Penn Square and the Park* urged a direct communication from Penn Square to the neighborhood of Girard Avenue Bridge. In 1884 one C. K. Landis, the founder of Vineland, N.J., published a drawing showing a wide boulevard from City Hall to the present site of the museum as an entrance to the park. This is precisely the route of the present Benjamin Franklin Parkway.

The Parkway Association was organized in 1902 with John H. Converse of the Art Association as President. In 1903 the parkway was placed on the City Plan and in the following year $2,000,000 was appropriated for parkway purposes. In 1907 the Art Association appointed a commission consisting of Paul P. Cret, Clarence C. Zantzinger, and Horace Trumbauer to

PLATE 58.   Ellen Phillips Samuel Memorial. *The Immigrant* in foreground.

PLATE 59. Ellen Phillips Samuel Memorial. *The Sentry*.

study the parkway problem and submit a plan. Such a plan was prepared and was essentially the plan of the present parkway. That plan was further developed by Jacques Gréber of Paris, France, in 1917.

Another project in city planning sponsored by the Art Association and the Independence Hall Association is the Independence Hall Mall, designed by the late Roy F. Larson, who once told me he considered it to be the finest thing he had done.

The dream of Charles Howell and Henry Fox over a hundred years ago of the Fairmount Park Art Association has come true in amazing and wonderful ways.

PLATE 60.   Ellen Phillips Samuel Memorial. *Settling of the Seaboard.*

PLATE 61. *Three Flying Figures.* Carl Milles, sculptor. Bower and Fradley, architects.

PLATE 62. *John B. Kelly, oarsman.* Harry Rosen, sculptor.

PLATE 63. Frederick Graff Memorial.

PLATE 64. *Marquis de Lafayette.* Raoul Josset, sculptor.

PLATE 65. Lincoln Monument. Randolph Rogers, sculptor.

Appendix

**First Board of Managers
Zoological Society of Philadelphia**

William Camac, M.D.
 President

James C. Hand,
 Vice-President

J. Gillingham Fell
 Vice-President

John L. LeConte, M.D.
 Corresponding Secretary

John L. Ridgeway
 Recording Secretary

Frank H. Clark
 Treasurer

Managers
William S. Vaux

Frederick Graff
George W. Childs
J. Vaughn Merrick
John Wagner
William H. Merrick
S. Fisher Corlies
Theodore L. Harrison
Henry C. Gibson
Issac J. Wistar
Edward Biddle
Charles Norris

**Present Board of Directors
Zoological Society of Philadelphia**

John G. Williams
 Chairman

Richard W. Foster
 Vice-Chairman

James D. Winsor, III
 Vice-Chairman

122

Ronald T. Reuther
    President

Antelo Devereux
    Secretary-Treasurer

I. Tatnall Starr, II
    Assistant Secretary-Treasurer

Directors

Dr. James H. Birnie
Bennett Blum
Alan Crawford, Jr.
G. Kurt Davidyan
R. M. deSchauensee
Frank H. Goodyear
Maurice Heckscher
James M. Large
Henry D. Mirick
Frank Palumbo
John A. Philbrick, 3rd
Mrs. Steward Rauch, Jr.
Robin E. Roberts
Mrs. Isador M. Scott
George F. Tyler, Jr.
Harry F. West
Richard D. Wood
Charles H. Woodward
John W. York

Ex Officio

Hon. Frank L. Rizzo, Mayor
George X. Schwartz, President,
    City Council
Robert W. Crawford, President,
    Fairmount Park Commission

First Fairmount Park Commission

Morton McMichael, Mayor
    President

Joseph F. Mercer
    President of Common Council

Charles Dixey
    Commissioner of City Property

Strickland Kneass
    Engineer and Surveyer

Frederick Graff
    Engineer of Water Works

The following citizens:

Eli K. Price
John Welsh
William Sellers
Joseph Harrison, Jr.
John C. Cresson
Nathaniel B. Browne
Theodore Cuyler
Henry M. Phillips
Gustavus Remak
Maj. Gen. George G. Meade

First Board of Trustees
Fairmount Park Art Association

Anthony J. Drexel
    President

H. Corbit Ogden
    Vice-President

James L. Claghorn
    Treasurer

John Bellangee Cox
    Secretary

Edward H. Trotter
William J. Horstmann
Henry C. Gibson
Samuel S. White
Henry K. Fox
Charles H. Howell
Thomas Dolan
Archibald Campbell

Bibliography

Academy of Natural Sciences of Philadelphia. Proceedings. April 1910.

Brinton, Mary Williams. *Their Lives and Mine*. Philadelphia: Privately Printed, 1972.

Cadwalader, Williams Biddle. *Philadelphia's Zoo*. Philadelphia: Newcomen Society of North America, 1949.

Chadwick, F. *The Park and the Town*. New York: Frederick A. Praeger, 1973.

Daly, T. A. *The Wissahickon*. Philadelphia: Garden Club of Philadelphia, 1922.

Earle, Sidney M. "Fairmount Park, History to 1950." Manuscript, Historical Society of Pennsylvania.

Fairmount Park Art Association. *Fiftieth Anniversary, 1921*.

Keyser, Charles S. *Fairmount Park*. Philadelphia: Claxton, Remsen and Haffelfinger, 1871.

Library Company of Philadelphia. Reports of Fairmount Park Commission, 1867-1868.

Library of Congress. *Olmsted Papers*.

Marceau. Henri. Seventy-fifth Annual Report, Fairmount Park Art Association, 1946.

Philadelphia Archives. Proceedings of the Fairmount Park Commission from 1867.

Sutton, Silvia B. *Olmsted*. Cambridge, Mass.: M.I.T. Press, 1973.

Tatum, George B. *Penn's Great Town*. Philadelphia: University of Pennsylvania Press, 1961.

Zoological Society of Philadelphia. Proceedings and WPA History by Gracey, 1940.

Index

Numbers in italics refer to illustrations.